The Great Retirement Escape

Your Guide to Journeys Across the Globe, Adventures Close to Home, Inspiring Outdoor Activities, and Fun Active Lifestyle for Your Best Years Yet

Lara West

Copyright © 2024 by Lara West

The content contained within this book may not be reproduced, duplicated, stored in a retrieval system, or transmitted in any form or by any means, electronic, mechanical, photocopying, recording, or otherwise, without direct written permission from the author or the publisher.

Legal Notice:

This book is copyright-protected. It is only for personal use. You cannot amend, distribute, sell, use, quote, or paraphrase any part, or the content within this book, without the consent of the author or publisher.

Disclaimer Notice:

Please note the information contained within this book is for educational and entertainment purposes only. All readers/viewers of this content are advised to consult their doctors or qualified health professionals regarding specific health questions before beginning any fitness or lifestyle program.

The content within this book has been derived from various sources. All effort has been executed to present accurate, up-to-date, reliable, and complete information. No warranties of any kind are declared or implied. Readers acknowledge that the author is not engaged in the rendering of legal, medical, or professional advice. Neither Lara West nor the publisher takes any responsibility for possible health consequences of any person reading or following the information in this educational content.

By reading this document, the reader agrees that under no circumstances is the author responsible for any losses, direct or indirect, that are incurred as a result of the use of the information contained within this document, including, but not limited to, errors, omissions, or inaccuracies.

Contents

1. Introduction — 1
2. Designing Your Dream Retirement: A Blueprint for Adventure and Fulfillment — 4

   2.1 Charting Your Path to an Epic Retirement Adventure

   2.2 Maximizing Your Adventures with Minimal Spending

   2.3 Essential Digital Tools for Modern Retirees

   2.4 Balancing Safety with Adventure

3. Pathways to Wellness: Inspiring Journeys for a Healthy and Active Retirement — 22

   3.1 Finding Peace: Mindfulness and Meditation Retreats

   3.2 Golf as a Social Game: Connection, Fitness, and Fun

   3.3 Refreshing Waters: Water Aerobics, Swimming, and Cold Plunges

   3.4 Floating into Wellness: The Sensory Deprivation Experience

   3.5 Fitness at Home: Online Classes and Resources

   3.6 Gardening for Fitness, Mindfulness, and Growth

   3.7 Tai Chi and Qigong: Gentle Movements for Strength and Balance

    3.8 Paddling to Health: Kayaking, Canoeing, and Paddleboarding

    3.9 Nordic Walking: A Whole-Body Approach to Staying Active

    3.10 Leisurely Rides: Scenic Biking Routes for Casual Cyclists

    3.11 Cross-Country Skiing: A Workout for Winter Wellness

    3.12 Cooking for Health: Fun Workshops and Classes

    3.13 Relax, Renew, Rebalance: Spa and Hot Springs Escapes

4. The World at Your Fingertips: Senior-Friendly Destinations, Budgets, and Beyond   49

    4.1 The Best Senior-Friendly Travel Destinations Worldwide

    4.2 The Best Travel Times for an Unforgettable Experience

    4.3 Group Travel: Finding Retirement Travel Clubs

    4.4 Solo Travel: Exploring the World on Your Own Terms

    4.5 A Comprehensive Guide to Traveling with Physical Limitations

    4.6 Seeing the World Without Breaking the Bank

5. Epic Journeys of a Lifetime: Unforgettable Travel Experiences   65

    5.1 Eco-Tourism: Environmentally Conscious Travel

    5.2 Voluntourism: Combining Travel with Volunteer Work

    5.3 Senior Safari Adventures: Planning the Trip of a Lifetime

    5.4 Sea Voyages and River Cruises: Unlocking Unforgettable Adventures

    5.5 Top Historical Landmarks for Your Global Bucket List

    5.6 Cultural European Tours for the Curious Retiree

    5.7 Learning While Traveling: Cultural Exchange Programs

    5.8 Savoring the World Through Food and Wine Adventures

6. Sky High & Deep Dive: Adventure-Fueled Experiences   94
   6.1 Skydiving and Paragliding: Thrills in the Sky
   6.2 Scuba Diving: Exploring Underwater Worlds
   6.3 Motorcycle Road Trips: On the Open Road with Confidence
   6.4 Hot Air Balloon Rides: Seeing the World from Above
   6.5 White Water Rafting: Riding the Waves of Adventure
   6.6 Mountain Biking for the Energetic Retiree
   6.7 Soaring Through the Skies with Zip-Lining

7. The Great Outdoors: Exploring Nature's Wonders   111
   7.1 Bird-Watching: Connecting with Nature's Winged Wonders
   7.2 Fishing and Boating: Relaxing by the Water
   7.3 Exploring the Wonders of National Parks
   7.4 Hidden Treasures: The Exciting World of Treasure Hunting
   7.5 Camping and Glamping: Relaxing Outdoor Retreats
   7.6 Charting the Course: Planning Your Dream RV Adventure
   7.7 Horseback Riding: Essentials for a Safe and Enjoyable Experience
   7.8. Exploring the Night Sky: Stargazing and Astronomy Clubs

8. Conclusion   127

Share Your Adventure and Inspire Others   129

About the Author   130

Resources   132
   Chapter 2.

Chapter 3.

Chapter 4.

Chapter 5.

Chapter 6.

Chapter 7.

References	149
Also by Lara West	154

1
Introduction

So, you've finally done it. You've handed over the keys to the office, given the farewell speech, either tearfully endless or joyfully brief, and walked out into the brave new world of retirement. This is the moment you've been waiting for, but now what? Are you supposed to sit on a porch swing and count the days like you're waiting for the end credits to roll? Hardly! Retirement is not the end of the road; it's the start of an exhilarating adventure. As you embark on this exciting journey, allow me to be your guide to help you navigate the twists and turns, uncover new passions, and fully embrace the limitless possibilities that lie ahead. Together, we'll explore how to make this chapter the most fulfilling and vibrant time of your life.

But first, let me introduce myself. I'm a woman in my early 60s, a business owner, a wife, and a mother. I adore my life, family, and business. I'm very active and always hungry for new experiences. And I plan to keep it that way throughout my 60s, 70s, and beyond. My husband, in his mid-60s, shares my enthusiasm for art, music, sports, travel, and intellectual pursuits. Together, we're committed to living a vibrant and adventurous life, and we will not let something as trivial as retirement slow us down. In fact, during one of those epiphany moments—when friends around us started retiring—I realized I wanted more freedom in our retirement years, soaking up every bit of joy, adventure, and creativity that retirement years offer. As I delved into what "retire" truly meant, I realized it was never something nature intended for us. The word itself, rooted in stepping back or withdrawing, didn't sit right with me. I didn't want to withdraw from life as I aged; I wanted to embrace it more fully. That's when I started devouring books, articles, and every piece of research I could find on making the most of this new chapter. What I found was electrifying. I discovered that retirement offered the opportunity for more joy, adventure, and creativity than at any other time in my life. And I knew I had to share this with others. Nature didn't design us to fade away; it designed us to grow, to flourish, and to live with purpose. Retirement, as I see it, is the beginning of a time to truly thrive.

This book is a result of my journey into planning for a fulfilling retirement. Its purpose is simple: to provide you with a joyful, creative, and adventurous roadmap for your retirement. We'll explore a wide variety of activities that cater to different interests, physical abilities, and budgets. From adrenaline-pumping adventures to serene, soul-soothing hobbies, there's something here for everyone. And don't worry, there's not a single mundane or trivial suggestion in sight.

As I began gathering information for this book, I realized something exciting. I had collected so much valuable content—enough to fill two books! Rather than overwhelm you with everything at once, I split the material into two separate books. This way, each can focus more deeply on specific areas of life in retirement.

The book you're holding now is dedicated to travel, outdoor adventures, health, and staying active—all the physical and adventurous pursuits that keep life exciting and fulfilling. Whether you're dreaming of exploring new destinations, hiking beautiful landscapes, or keeping your body and mind sharp through fitness, this book is your ultimate guide to making the most of your time outdoors and on the move.

I understand that not everyone may be solely interested in physical adventure or travel. That's why the second book, *Retirement Reinvented: Your Inspiring Guide to Creative Expression, Intellectual Growth, Entrepreneurial Ventures, and Leaving a Legacy for a Fulfilling and Meaningful Life After Work,* focuses on intellectual pursuits, creative expression, community building, and entrepreneurship—perfect for those looking to continue growing, learning, and connecting in meaningful ways. Each book offers a unique approach to thriving in retirement, allowing you to choose the path that speaks to you most.

But why limit yourself to one? For the most well-rounded and enriching retirement experience, I encourage you to explore both books. Together, they will create a complete guide to living a life filled with adventure, growth, and lasting connections. Whether you're drawn to outdoor exploration, the quiet satisfaction of creative and intellectual engagement, or both, these books will inspire you to make the most of this exciting chapter.

So, here's my call to action: approach your retirement with an adventurous spirit. Be open-minded and be willing to try new things. Use this book as your guide to explore the multitude of options available. To make these golden years the best years yet, let's redefine the idea of retirement. Let's think of retirement not as an end, but as a fantastic beginning. Let's embrace these years with enthusiasm and make them truly unforgettable. Buckle up; it's going to be a fantastic ride! Let's go!

2

Designing Your Dream Retirement: A Blueprint for Adventure and Fulfillment

You know that feeling when you walk into a room and forget why you're there? Well, that's how some folks approach retirement—except the room is the rest of your life, and you're not entirely sure what to do next. But let's flip that script. Picture yourself waking up every day, filled with anticipation of the possibility of starting a new hobby, meeting interesting people, or finally visiting your dream location. Sounds thrilling, right? That's what planning your adventure-filled retirement is all about.

2.1 Charting Your Path to an Epic Retirement Adventure

Define Bold and Clear Goals

Defining clear objectives for your retirement is like plotting a course for a fabulous journey. Start by identifying your passions and interests. Are you a thrill-seeker who's always wanted to sky dive, or do you find joy in more serene pursuits like painting or gardening? Creating a retirement bucket list can be a fun way to get started. Jot down everything you've ever wanted to do—no matter how outlandish it seems. Then, try visualizing a typical day in your retirement. Are you strolling through a local farmer's market or taking a cooking class in Tuscany? These exercises help bring your goals into sharper focus.

Once you have a list of potential goals, it's time to prioritize them. Not all dreams are created equal—some may be more workable than others, based on your resources and physical abilities. Rank your goals by considering what excites you the most, what's achievable given your current situation, and what aligns best with your long-term plans. This ranking helps maintain focus and motivation, ensuring that your most cherished dreams don't get lost in the shuffle.

Setting SMART Goals

Setting SMART goals is crucial in making your retirement dreams a reality. SMART stands for **Specific, Measurable, Achievable, Relevant, and Time-bound**. By breaking your goals down into these components, you create a clear path toward success. Let's explore each element in more detail with examples to help you create well-structured, attainable goals.

- **Specific:** The first step is to make your goal clear and specific. A vague goal like "I want to stay active" doesn't provide direction or motivation. Instead, try to specify exactly what you want to achieve. For example, "I want to walk 10,000 steps every day" or "I want to swim for one hour three times a week" makes it crystal clear what you're aiming for. Another example: instead of "I want to volunteer," try "I want to volunteer at the local animal shelter for five hours a week."

- **Measurable:** To know if you're making progress, your goals need to be measurable. This means putting numbers or milestones on your goals so you can track your advancement. Instead of saying "I want to read more books," make it measurable: "I want to read 24 books this year." This allows you to track your progress (two books per month) and celebrate small wins along the way. If you want to improve your fitness, set a measurable goal like "I want to lower my cholesterol to below 200 in six months."

- **Achievable**: While it's great to aim high, your goals should also be realistic and achievable given your circumstances. For example, if you've never hiked before, a goal of climbing Mount Kilimanjaro next year will be unrealistic. A more achievable goal would be "I want to hike five beginner trails this year." This way, you're pushing yourself instead of setting up for disappointment. Keep in mind your current health, time, and resources, and make sure your goals fit within those constraints.

- **Relevant**: Your goals should align with your overall vision for retirement and your personal interests. Ask yourself if the goal is meaningful and whether it brings you closer to your broader objectives. For example, if your broader vision is to stay socially engaged, a goal like "I want to take a photography class" may not align as well as "I want to join a photography club where I can meet new people." Ensuring your goals are relevant to your values will make them more motivating and worthwhile.

- **Time-bound**: Finally, always attach a timeline to your goals. Without deadlines, it's easy to procrastinate or lose motivation. Instead of saying "I want to learn a new language," try "I want to complete an introductory Italian course within the next six months." This gives you a sense of urgency and a clear deadline to work towards. A time-bound goal like "I want to complete a 5K run in the next three months" gives you a reason to stay committed.

Creating SMART goals will not only give your retirement plans structure but also boost your motivation and chances of success. Whether it's traveling, volunteering, learning a new skill, or improving your health, SMART goals provide a framework to turn your dreams into reality. By being specific, measuring your progress, setting achievable targets, ensuring relevance, and giving yourself deadlines, you'll be well on your way to a fulfilling and adventurous retirement!

Visualization Techniques

Visualization techniques can be incredibly powerful in turning your retirement dreams into reality. A vision board is a great tool for this. Grab some magazines, scissors, and glue, and start cutting out images and words that represent your goals. Arrange them on a board where you can see them every day. If you prefer a digital approach, there are plenty of free apps that make it easy to create a virtual vision board. Apps like **Canva, Pinterest,** and **Adobe Spark** allow you to gather images, words, and inspirational quotes that resonate with your goals. Simply drag and drop your selections onto a digital canvas, and arrange them in a way that feels meaningful to you. Whether you choose a traditional board or a digital one, the key is to place it somewhere you'll see it every day. This constant visual reminder helps keep your aspirations at the forefront of your mind.

Journaling is another effective technique that can help turn your retirement dreams into actionable steps. Start by writing down your retirement goals, but don't stop there. Dive deeper by creating detailed descriptions of what achieving each goal would look and feel like. Imagine the sights, sounds, fragrances, and emotions associated with your ideal retirement life. For instance, if your goal is to travel more, describe the destinations you want to visit, the experiences you hope to have, and the sense of adventure and fulfillment that comes with exploring unknown places. This kind of vivid writing brings your aspirations to life, making them more tangible and real.

Setting clear, prioritized, and achievable goals is the first step toward a retirement filled with adventure and fulfillment. These practices can provide a motivational boost when you need it most. Whether you're dreaming of skydiving, painting, or traveling, having a well-defined and emotionally charged plan can make those dreams a reality. Pour a cup of coffee, or a glass of wine, grab that pen or laptop, and get ready to create a dream plan to embark on the most exciting chapter of your life!

2.2 Maximizing Your Adventures with Minimal Spending

Assess Financial Resources

Let's face it, the idea of a retirement filled with endless adventures sounds delightful until you start thinking about the price tag. But don't worry, you can have your cake and eat it too. The first step is to assess your financial resources. Start by taking a thorough inventory of your savings, investments, and retirement accounts. If you have a pension, Social Security benefits, or income from rental properties, be sure to include these as well. It's also important to consider any potential sources of income you might tap into during retirement, such as part-time work, consulting, or freelancing. Take a realistic look at what you're spending now and how it might change when you retire. Will you downsize your home? Travel more? By understanding all of your financial resources, you can form a picture of what's feasible and prioritize your spending on the activities that matter most to you. To simplify this process, consider working with a financial advisor or using online retirement calculators like those available through **Fidelity** or **Vanguard** to give you a clearer idea of your retirement income potential.

Create a Retirement Budget

Creating a retirement budget is the next logical step after assessing your financial resources. While this may sound tedious, think of it as your roadmap to financial freedom during retirement—it's how you'll ensure you're living comfortably while still having enough to fund those dream vacations or new hobbies. Start by listing your **fixed expenses**, such as rent or mortgage payments, property taxes, utilities, groceries, and healthcare costs. Keep in mind that healthcare can become a larger expense as you age, so you may want to allocate a generous portion of your budget to medical care and insurance premiums.

Next, consider your **variable expenses**, which include things like dining out, entertainment, hobbies, travel, and any new recreational activities you plan to pick up during retirement. It's important to strike a balance between your everyday needs and the things that bring you joy. This is where budgeting gets fun—you can earmark a portion of your income for adventures and hobbies that enhance your life. Want to take an annual vacation or buy a new camera for your photography hobby? Include those in your budget!

When drafting your budget, don't forget to include an **emergency fund** for unexpected costs like home repairs or medical emergencies. This safety net can help prevent financial stress when life throws an unexpected curveball. Consider using financial planning tools to track your expenses, visualize your budget, and help you stay on course. With a well-planned budget, you can enjoy your retirement without worrying about overspending—allowing you to live large while keeping your finances in check.

Financial Planning Tools

Financial planning tools can be incredibly useful for planning and keeping your finances in check. Apps like **Rocket Money, You Need a Budget (YNAB), Empower (formerly Personal Capital), Simplifi, PocketSmith, and Tiller** can help you manage your funds more effectively. These tools allow you to track your spending, set financial goals, and even get alerts when you're veering off course. It's like having a financial advisor in your pocket, minus the hefty fees. By leveraging these resources, you can ensure your funds are allocated wisely, allowing you to indulge in adventures without financial stress.

Cost-Saving Tips for Retirees

Now, who doesn't love a good bargain? Cost-saving tips for activities can help you stretch your dollars further, sacrificing none of the fun. The first and easiest step is to take full advantage of **senior discounts**. These perks are available in more places than you might think. From discounts at local theaters, movie cinemas, and restaurants to reduced rates for public transportation and museums, every little savings can add up over time. For instance, **AARP (**American Association of Retired Persons) and other senior organizations often offer special discounts at hotels, car rental companies, and even retail stores, making membership a great investment. Please refer to the **Resources Chapter** for a list of organizations offering worldwide resources, advocacy, services, and discounts for seniors.

Another savvy strategy is to plan your trip during **off-peak or shoulder seasons**. Traveling just before or after peak tourist times allows you to save money on flights, accommodations, and attractions while avoiding the crowds. For instance, visiting popular European cities in early spring or late autumn often results in lower costs and a more relaxed experience. Tools like **Google Flights, Skyscanner**, and **Kayak** can help you find the best deals on flights, especially if you're flexible with your travel dates. Booking mid-week can sometimes save you a significant amount on airfare as well.

When it comes to accommodations, consider alternatives like **Airbnb** for longer stays, as they often offer better rates than hotels. However, don't overlook the benefits of contacting hotels directly, as many now offer lower rates when booked through their websites. Some hotels might even throw in extras like free breakfast or room upgrades. **Hostels** can also be a great option—they aren't just for backpackers anymore! Many now offer private rooms at affordable rates.

Using price comparison websites is a powerful tool for saving money on everything from flights to accommodations. Websites like **Google Flights, Skyscanner, and Kayak** allow you to compare prices across different airlines and booking platforms, helping you find the best deals on airfare. By setting up alerts for price drops, you can track fluctuations and book your tickets when rates are at their lowest. Similarly, for accommodations, platforms like **Booking.com, Airbnb, and Hotels.com** offer comprehensive searches that let you filter by price, amenities, and reviews. When booking car rentals, **Rentalcars.com** and **Expedia** can help you compare prices across multiple rental agencies, ensuring you get the best deal. With a few clicks, you can quickly evaluate options and make informed choices that save you time, effort, and money—leaving more in your budget for those unforgettable experiences.

For activities, **local attractions** can offer fantastic budget-friendly entertainment. Check out free or low-cost events like community festivals or outdoor concerts. Many museums and galleries offer free admission days or senior discounts. Nature lovers can take full advantage of **hiking trails, parks, and nature reserves**, often free or requiring only a small entrance fee. For example, in the U.S., you can purchase a **National Parks Senior Pass**, granting lifetime access to over 2,000 national parks and recreation sites for a one-time fee. This is perfect for nature lovers who want to explore hiking trails, parks, and reserves without constantly worrying about entrance fees.

For meals, **eating like a local** is key to saving money and experiencing the true flavor of a place. Avoid touristy restaurants and opt for local markets, street food, or eateries where the locals dine. Not only are they more affordable, but they also offer a more authentic culinary experience. Shop for breakfast items or snacks at local grocery stores to cut down on dining costs.

Technology is your best friend when traveling on a budget. Apps like **Hopper** can predict the best time to book flights, while **HotelTonight** offers last-minute accommodation deals. Digital maps, such as **Google Maps**, can help you navigate new cities with no need for pricey guided tours—simply create your own route with points of interest, hidden gems, and local eateries.

Another option to save on recreational activities is to join **local clubs or community centers**. Many offer low-cost or free classes and workshops in activities such as painting, dancing, or gardening. These are not only budget-friendly but also a great way to socialize and make new friends who share your interests.

Take advantage of online resources and apps like **Meetup.com** or **Eventbrite** to find free events and gatherings in your area. Whether it's a group hiking trip, a photography workshop, or a book club meeting, these platforms are treasure troves of budget-friendly activities that can enrich your retirement experience. With a bit of planning and creativity, you can enjoy an active and fulfilling retirement without breaking the bank.

To illustrate, let's take a real-life example. When my husband and I decided to take a month-long trip to Europe, we didn't want to drain our savings. We started by creating a detailed budget, allocating funds for flights, accommodations, and daily expenses. Then we booked flights during the off-peak season and took advantage of senior discounts on car rentals. We found great deals on **Booking.com**, allowing us to stay in lovely, affordable accommodations. We also stayed a few times in charming and budget-friendly Airbnb rentals. By using **Rocket Money** to track our spending daily, we managed to stick to our budget without sacrificing experiences. The result? A fantastic, memorable trip that didn't break the bank.

So, as you can see, maximizing your adventures with minimal spending is entirely possible. With careful planning, smart budgeting, and a little creativity, you can make your retirement dreams a reality without financial stress.

2.3 Essential Digital Tools for Modern Retirees

Basic Technology Skills

So, you've packed away the office supplies, handed over your work badge, and are ready to embrace retirement. No more after-hours calls and deadline emails! But don't toss that smartphone and tablet aside just yet! These gadgets are about to become your best retirement friends. First, let's talk about mastering the basics. You might think you know your way around a smartphone, but do you? Can you download apps and use them fast and efficiently? How comfortable are you navigating the app store to find new tools to enhance your day-to-day life? Can you manage different social media platforms like Facebook or Instagram (they keep changing all the time) to stay connected with friends and family? Do you know how to troubleshoot when something goes awry? Understanding how to reset your device, update software, or fix common glitches will save you from unnecessary frustration.

Beyond these, there are a few more tech-related questions to ask yourself. Are you familiar with cloud storage? With photos, documents, and apps accumulating on your devices, learning to use cloud services like **Google Drive or iCloud** can ensure your files are safe and accessible from anywhere. Do you know how to maximize your device's security settings? Keeping your data safe with strong passwords and two-factor authentication is essential.

To answer these questions and build your skills, start by doing some research. Search for online tutorials and videos on platforms like **YouTube**, which have step-by-step guides on everything from basic smartphone use to more advanced troubleshooting. Websites like **TechBoomers** and **Seniors Guide to Computers** offer free courses specifically designed for older adults wanting to boost their tech literacy. You can also explore free courses on **Udemy** or **Coursera** that cover smartphone and tablet basics. By taking advantage of these resources, you'll be mastering your devices and apps in no time, making your retirement both connected and exciting.

Technology for Travel and Leisure

Learning to use navigation apps like **Google Maps, Apple Maps, MapQuest, Waze, CoPilot GPS, RoadTrippers, Alltrails, and Citymapper** (for public transportation) can turn a simple walk in the park into an exciting treasure hunt for new places to explore. Just type in your destination, and you're off on a smooth, worry-free journey.

There's nothing like the thrill of dreaming up and booking your next adventure. But without the right prep, that excitement can fade fast. Thankfully, we've got travel apps to save the day. They cover everything, from trip planning **(GoogleTravel, TripCase, Wanderlog)** to booking attractions **(Viator, Steller, Culture Trip)**, flights, hotels, or rental cars **(Hopper, HotelTonight, TripAdvisor, Airbnb, Booking.com, Expedia, Hotels.com, Kayak, VRBO)**, to currency conversions

(Xe), to dining **(WorldofMouth, OpenTable, EatWith)**, making trips smoother and more budget-friendly and helping you find unique accommodations and hidden gems in any city.

And for the bookworms out there, an e-reader apps like the **Kindle, Google Play Books, Apple Books, Nook, Kobo, and Libby** can store thousands of books, offering endless entertainment without the bulk. Imagine sitting by a serene lake, or on a transatlantic flight, flipping through the latest bestseller on your e-reader. Pure bliss.

Staying Connected

Staying connected has never been easier, thanks to technology. Platforms like **Skype and Zoom** have become indispensable, especially for those of us with family and friends scattered across the globe. A quick video call can bridge the miles, making it feel like your loved ones are right there with you. Social media platforms like **Facebook, WhatsApp, and X (formerly Twitter)** offer a fantastic way to stay updated with what's happening in your friends' and family's lives. Sharing photos **(KwikPic, Instagram, Google Photos)**, commenting on posts, and even creating your own retirement blog **(Squarespace, Wix, Pixpa, Blogger, Hostinger, BTW)** can keep you engaged and socially active.

Health Management Apps

Health management is another area where technology shines. With the plethora of health and wellness apps available, managing your health has never been more convenient. Apps like **MyFitnessPal, Noom, FIIT** can help you track your diet and exercise routines, while others like **Medisafe** remind you to take your medications on time. **HealthTap** provides a personalized answer from doctors in less than 24 hours. **Headspace, Calm, and Insight Timer** have hundreds of guided meditations. And **Apple Fitness Plus, BetterMe, Glo, and SWEAT** track your progress and help you learn new workouts.

Fitness trackers, such as **Fitbit, Apple Watch, and Oura Ring**, monitor your steps, heart rate, and even your sleep patterns. These gadgets can be particularly useful for staying on top of your health goals. Imagine going for your morning walk, glancing at your wrist, and seeing that you've already hit your step goal for the day. It's a small but satisfying victory that keeps you motivated.

As you can see, digital tools can truly enhance your retirement, helping you stay close to loved ones, manage your health, and make the most of your travels. But remember, while these gadgets and apps are great, it's just as important to take time away from the screen. Balance is key—use technology to enrich your life, but don't forget to unplug and savor the moments that make your life special. Power up when you need to, and also make sure to set the devices aside and enjoy the sights and sounds of the world around you.

2.4 Balancing Safety with Adventure

Routine Medical Check-ups

Let's talk about the tightrope walk of balancing safety with adventure. First and foremost, routine medical check-ups are non-negotiable. Think of them as the pit stops on your grand adventure. Regular visits to your healthcare provider ensure you catch any potential issues early, keeping you on the road to a healthy retirement. Discuss your physical activities and future plans with your doctor to ensure they are safe for your specific health conditions. This proactive approach not only maintains your health but also gives you peace of mind, knowing you're fit to tackle whatever adventure comes your way.

Risk Assessment for Activities

Not all of us are in peak physical condition, and that's perfectly okay. The key is adapting activities to match your physical abilities. If hiking up a mountain sounds daunting, opt for a nature walk on a flat trail. Love the idea of cycling but worried about balance? Consider an electric bike. Swimming can be gentle laps in a pool instead of battling ocean waves. If getting on the floor is challenging, you can do chair yoga. There are always modifications and alternatives available, ensuring you can still take part in activities that bring you joy. The goal is to stay active in a way that is safe and feels good to you.

Now picture this: you're all set to hike up a scenic trail, your backpack is stocked, your boots are laced, and then it dawns on you—what if something goes wrong? Don't let that thought send you diving under the covers. Instead, let's tackle risk assessment head-on. Start by considering the activity at hand. Hiking, for example, might seem straightforward but involves risks like uneven terrain, weather changes, and wildlife encounters. Assess the difficulty level of the trail and your fitness level. Ask yourself, do you have the stamina for a five-mile hike, or should you start with something shorter?

If you're planning to travel abroad, research your destination. Know the local customs, understand the political climate, and be aware of any health advisories and the necessary vaccines. For example, in some countries, it's crucial to avoid certain areas after dark, or perhaps it's customary to dress modestly. These minor adjustments can make a big difference. Consider other potential risks like natural disasters, unfamiliar legal systems, and the possibility of scams or petty crime. Knowledge isn't just power—it's your ticket to a safe and enjoyable adventure.

Safety Measures and Emergency Preparedness

Safety measures and precautions are your best friends when it comes to enjoying activities without the looming shadow of danger. For instance, if you're into cycling, wearing a helmet isn't just a good idea; it's a must. Invest in good-quality gear—from helmets and gloves to reflective clothing. And don't forget to check your bike's brakes and tires before hitting the road. If you're planning on cycling long distances, consider carrying a small repair kit that includes tire patches, a multi-tool, and a portable pump. For night rides, make sure to have proper lights—both front and rear—to ensure visibility to others on the road.

When trying out new sports, following your instructor's advice is critical. Whether it's scuba diving, rock climbing, or skiing, these experts know their stuff, and following their guidance can prevent mishaps. Ask questions if you're unsure about a technique or piece of equipment. Get familiar with the terrain and weather conditions before heading out, especially for activities or areas where the environment can change unexpectedly.

Safety is key to enjoying a road trip without unexpected hassles. Before you hit the road, make sure your car is in top shape. Check the oil, tires, and brakes, and don't forget to ensure your spare tire is ready for action. Pack an emergency kit with essentials like a first aid kit, flashlight, jumper cables, and extra water. For longer trips, include a portable battery charger for your devices, a blanket, and extra snacks.

It's also essential to keep a friend or family member informed about your travel plans. Before heading out, share your route, accommodations, and general itinerary with someone back home. Check in regularly, especially if you're moving between different locations. For longer trips or more adventurous travel, consider using a location-sharing app like **Google Maps** or **Find My Friends** so loved ones can track your whereabouts in real time. This way, if you experience any unexpected changes or delays, someone will know your general location and can raise an alert if necessary. It's an extra layer of security that gives both you and your family peace of mind during your travels.

For all activities, don't underestimate the importance of staying hydrated and applying sunscreen, even on cloudy days or when engaging in water sports. Having a reliable first-aid kit and basic first aid knowledge can also come in handy, whether you're hiking, camping, or simply spending a day at the beach.

Emergency preparedness is the foundation of safe adventuring. Picture yourself hiking on a beautiful trail when you twist your ankle—what's your plan? Being prepared for these situations can make all the difference. Always carry a well-stocked first aid kit, whether you're hiking, biking, or traveling. Your kit should include essentials like adhesive bandages, antiseptic wipes, gauze, medical tape, pain relievers, and blister pads. It's equally important to know the basics of first aid: how to clean and dress a wound, properly bandage a sprain, and recognize signs of dehydration or heatstroke. Having these skills ensures you can handle minor injuries on the spot and prevent them from becoming bigger issues.

Besides your first aid kit, make sure to have a list of local emergency contacts handy. If you're traveling abroad, familiarize yourself with the local emergency services number—the equivalent of 911—so you can act quickly in a crisis. It's also a good idea to store important numbers, like your doctor's, your travel insurance company's, and the nearest embassy or consulate, in both your phone and on paper, in case your phone dies or gets lost.

To prevent being left in a vulnerable situation with a dead phone, carry a small power bank to ensure your device stays charged. A portable charger can be a lifesaver when you're out in nature or traveling in remote areas with no access to electricity. Having backup power ensures that you can make emergency calls, use offline maps, or access important information at any time.

Another smart move is to download offline maps and health-related apps, which can guide you to the nearest medical facility or help you find your way, even if you don't have cell service. But sometimes, technology can only take you so far, and an old-fashioned paper map can be a real lifesaver. I remember one time when my husband was mountain biking in a new area while I was hiking. We had no cellular service, and he ended up taking a wrong turn and getting lost. Fortunately, he had a trail map with him and used it to navigate his way back to the parking lot, where I had been waiting anxiously for what felt like ages. His paper map saved the day when digital tools couldn't. A funny fact: that area was around a lake on Vancouver Island called the Lost Lake, which we now call the "Lost and Found" Lake.

With these precautions in place—whether digital or traditional—a little foresight can turn a potential disaster into a manageable inconvenience, allowing you to continue your adventure safely and confidently.

When engaging in outdoor adventures, it's also essential to be prepared for potential encounters with wildlife. Whether you're hiking in a national park, camping, or exploring a remote trail, understanding the local fauna and how to react to encounters can ensure both your safety and the safety of the animals. Always research the wildlife in the area you're visiting, including any potential dangers like bears, mountain lions, or snakes. Carry bear spray in areas known for bear activity and store food properly in bear-proof containers or hang it from a tree to avoid attracting wildlife to your campsite. When hiking, make noise periodically to avoid surprising animals, especially in dense forests or near water sources. If you encounter wildlife, remain calm, keep your distance, and never approach or feed the animals. Many parks provide specific guidelines for handling wildlife encounters, so be sure to review these before heading out. Your awareness and preparedness can prevent dangerous situations while allowing you to peacefully enjoy the natural beauty of your surroundings.

Insurance and Legal Considerations

Now, let's talk about the not-so-glamorous but utterly crucial topic of insurance and legal considerations. Imagine you're on a dream vacation in Bali, and you suddenly need medical attention. Travel insurance can be a lifesaver, covering everything from medical emergencies to trip cancellations. Make sure your travel insurance includes medical evacuation—you don't want to be stuck with a hefty bill if you need to be flown back home. It should also cover any unexpected incidents like trip cancellations or lost luggage. Being prepared helps you focus on the excitement of your adventure rather than worrying about the "what-ifs."

For those engaging in activities like skiing or scuba diving, check if your insurance covers these high-risk activities. Medical insurance is equally important. Ensure you have a plan that covers regular check-ups and emergencies. And don't overlook legal considerations. If you're planning to drive in a foreign country, ensure you have the appropriate licenses and understand local driving laws. Ignorance isn't bliss when it comes to legal matters—it's a recipe for trouble.

Please refer to the **Resources Chapter** for insurance companies' recommendations.

As you plan your retirement adventures, remember that a bit of forethought and preparation can turn potential risks into manageable challenges. Embrace the thrill, but keep safety at the forefront. Your golden years are meant to be enjoyed, and a well-balanced approach ensures that every adventure is both exhilarating and safe.

3

Pathways to Wellness: Inspiring Journeys for a Healthy and Active Retirement

Retirement is the perfect time to focus on health and wellness, and there are countless ways to do so. Many people think that health and wellness are all about hitting the gym or sticking to a healthy diet, and while those are important, let's take a broader, more mindful approach. After all, no adventure, contribution, or new passion can truly flourish if your health is not in good shape. That's why I'm starting with this essential chapter on health and wellness—a strong foundation is key to enjoying all the experiences retirement has to offer. Without it, even the grandest travel plans or the most exciting new hobbies can become challenging. Taking time to invest in both your physical and mental well-being is crucial. In this chapter, we'll dive into mindfulness, movement, nutrition, and other wellness practices that can support you in improving and maintaining your health, bring peace to your mind, and joy to your heart so you can fully embrace this next chapter of life with vitality. Let's start with an often-overlooked, yet incredibly powerful, tool: mindfulness.

3.1 Finding Peace: Mindfulness and Meditation Retreats

Exploring the benefits of mindfulness and meditation is like opening a treasure chest of mental and physical health rewards. Imagine reducing stress so effectively that you forget what it even felt like in the first place. Mindfulness and meditation help you achieve just that. These practices improve focus, allowing you to savor each moment more fully. They also help with emotional regulation—suddenly, those little annoyances that once ruffled your feathers become as insignificant as a speck of dust. The benefits are scientifically backed, with many studies showing how mindfulness can lower blood pressure, reduce anxiety, and improve sleep quality.

Finding the right retreat is crucial. You don't want to end up in a place where the "meditation leader" is more interested in your wallet than in your well-being. Ensure the leaders are qualified; a good retreat will have experienced instructors with credentials in mindfulness and meditation practices, like Certified Mindfulness Teacher or Certified Mindfulness Informed Professional.

Look for retreats that offer a serene environment, whether it's a mountainside sanctuary or a peaceful beach resort. Activities should include guided meditations, yoga sessions, and some time for silent reflection. You might enjoy healthy cooking classes that focus on nourishing both body and mind or journaling workshops that help you explore your thoughts and emotions in a supportive environment. Nature walks, creative arts sessions, and mindful movement practices such as Tai Chi could also be part of the experience, offering a holistic approach to rejuvenation and inner peace.

There are many types of retreats, from weekend getaways to week-long immersions. Please refer to the **Resources Chapter** for some popular retreats known for their serene environments and experienced instructors.

Preparing for a retreat involves more than just packing your yoga pants and a comfy sweater. Mentally, approach the experience with an open mind and a heart ready to embrace tranquility. Physically, pack light but smart. Comfortable clothing is a must, along with any personal items that help you relax, like a scented candle, a favorite book, or a journal. Bring a reusable water bottle and some healthy snacks. Expect to disconnect from the digital world—most retreats encourage limited use of phones and other devices to help you immerse yourself fully in the experience.

Integrating practices into daily life ensures that the peace and focus you gain from the retreat don't fade away once you return home. Start with a daily routine; even five minutes of mindfulness each morning can set a positive tone for the day. Many apps, like **Headspace, Insight Timer, and Calm**, offer guided meditations perfect for beginners. Local community centers or yoga studios often provide mindfulness classes, allowing you to practice in a supportive environment. Over time, these practices can become as natural to you as brushing your teeth, providing lasting benefits for your mental and physical health.

3.2 Golf as a Social Game: Connection, Fitness, and Fun

So you pictured yourself on a lush green course, a gentle breeze on your face, and the satisfying sound of a well-struck ball, and you've decided to take up golf. Excellent choice! Golf is the perfect blend of exercise, relaxation, and social interaction. The game's beauty lies in its simplicity and complexity, making it engaging for newbies and seasoned players alike.

Let's start with the basics. First, understand the equipment. You'll need a set of golf clubs, which typically includes drivers, irons, wedges, and a putter. You don't need to buy the most expensive set. Beginners can start with a basic set and upgrade later as their skills improve. You'll also need balls, tees, and gloves—nothing too fancy at first, just the essentials to get started.

Understanding the basic rules and etiquette is equally important. Know when to be quiet, where to stand, and how to keep score. These small details contribute to the overall experience and enjoyment of the game, and they help maintain the respect and rhythm that golfers value.

A great way to kick-start your golfing journey is by taking beginner classes. Many golf courses and clubs offer lessons specifically designed for new players, where you'll learn proper technique, how to swing, and course strategies. Plus, an instructor can help you correct mistakes early on, making the learning process smoother and more enjoyable.

The physical benefits of golf are many. Walking the course improves muscle tone and balance without the jarring impact of more intense sports. Swinging the club engages various muscle groups and enhances flexibility. But it's not just about the body. Golf is a mental game, requiring concentration and strategic thinking. The serene outdoor environment also offers a pleasant break, allowing you to soak in nature while you play.

Golfers can adapt the game to suit their fitness levels. Not everyone can walk 18 holes, and that's okay. Golf carts are a great way to get around the course without overexerting yourself. If a full course seems too daunting, start with a shorter, 9-hole course. Senior-friendly equipment, like lighter clubs with larger grips, can make the game more accessible and enjoyable. These small adjustments ensure you can enjoy the game without straining your body, making it a lifelong sport.

One of the best aspects of golf is its social nature. Joining a local golf club can open up a world of new friendships and social opportunities. Many clubs offer group clinics, perfect for learning the game and meeting people. Weekly tournaments and social gatherings provide additional chances to mingle. Whether you're playing a round with old friends or joining a foursome with new acquaintances, golf offers countless opportunities for social interaction. And the clubhouse is always a great spot for post-game drinks and banter.

3.3 Refreshing Waters: Water Aerobics, Swimming, and Cold Plunges

There's something truly magical about being in the water, where every movement feels fluid and weightless. The gentle embrace of the water creates a sense of calm and freedom, offering a unique combination of relaxation and invigoration. When you're gliding effortlessly through the water, feeling the light resistance as you move, your joints thank you with every stroke. These activities provide a low-impact workout that's perfect for aging bodies. The buoyancy of the water reduces the stress on your joints and musculoskeletal system, making it an ideal exercise if you suffer from arthritis or other joint issues. The resistance water offers helps build strength and improve flexibility without the risk of injury that comes with high-impact exercises.

Pool-Based Water Aerobics and Swimming

Starting a water aerobics or swimming routine doesn't require much. Grab a comfortable swimsuit, water shoes for better traction, and a pair of goggles if you plan to swim laps. You might also want to invest in some pool noodles or water dumbbells to add variety to your workouts, however they are available in most pools. When you're in the water, safety is paramount. Make sure the pool has a lifeguard on duty and always inform someone of your swim schedule. Start slowly and gradually increase the intensity of your workouts as your body adapts. Whether you're doing structured water aerobics classes or swimming laps at your own pace, consistency is key to reaping the benefits.

Warm water exercises add another layer of benefit. Exercising in a heated pool can help relax muscles and ease joint pain, making your workout even more effective. The warmth also increases blood flow, aiding in quicker recovery post-exercise. Finding a pool that offers warm water sessions can be very beneficial if you deal with chronic pain or stiffness. Some community centers and health clubs have specific times when they heat their pools to cater to those needing that extra comfort.

Cold Water Swimming and Outdoor Plunges

For those seeking a more exhilarating experience, cold-water swimming and outdoor plunges offer a thrilling way to engage with nature while boosting overall health. Swimming in lakes, rivers, or the ocean adds an extra dimension of freedom compared to a pool environment. But it's the cold water that truly provides unique benefits—enhancing circulation, reducing inflammation, and even boosting mental clarity and resilience. Cold-water exposure has been linked to improved immune function and mood, making it a fantastic option for retirees looking to keep their bodies and minds sharp.

If you're ready to try cold-water swimming, safety is crucial. Start by ensuring you're familiar with the location—research local conditions and currents, and never swim alone. Gradually acclimate to cold water by starting with shorter dips and slowly increasing the duration as your body adjusts. Experts recommend beginning with water temperatures around 10-15°C (50-59°F), which can provide the benefits of cold exposure without overwhelming your system. Begin with brief dips lasting 10 to 30 seconds, and over time, you can work up to 1-2 minutes as your tolerance increases. It's important to always listen to your body and exit the water if you begin to feel too uncomfortable. Have warm, dry clothing ready when you exit the water to prevent excessive chilling, and consider using a wetsuit for longer swims.

The Finnish Sauna Tradition of Cold Plunges

For centuries, Finland and Russia have upheld the invigorating tradition of alternating between hot saunas and icy cold plunges. After spending time in the heat of a sauna, locals take a brief, shocking dip into a nearby frozen lake or a cold-water pool, embracing the sharp contrast in temperatures. This practice stimulates circulation, promotes deep relaxation, and even relieves chronic aches and pains, making it a perfect wellness ritual for retirees.

This tradition has expanded beyond the Nordic regions, and many modern wellness centers worldwide now offer these experiences. Facilities often provide sauna rooms paired with ice-cold plunge pools, allowing you to enjoy the therapeutic benefits without venturing into the wild. These sauna-and-plunge sessions are ideal for improving circulation, boosting the immune system, and enhancing mental clarity while providing a unique and rejuvenating experience.

If you're new to cold plunges, start by immersing yourself for no longer than 30 seconds to 1 minute in water temperatures ranging from 10-15°C (50-59°F). Gradually, you can increase the time as your body becomes accustomed to the cold.

Before incorporating cold-water plunges or outdoor swimming into your routine, consult with a healthcare provider, especially if you have any underlying health conditions like heart issues or respiratory problems. Cold exposure can be a shock to the system, so ensuring your body is ready for this practice will keep you safe while maximizing the health benefits.

3.4 Floating into Wellness: The Sensory Deprivation Experience

For those looking to explore a more meditative, introspective pathway to wellness in water, sensory deprivation floats offer a deeply relaxing and rejuvenating experience. When you're drifting effortlessly in a saltwater float pod, completely free of external distractions, your senses have a chance to rest and reset. The water, infused with high concentrations of Epsom salts, creates a buoyancy that makes you feel weightless, while the isolation chamber eliminates outside noise, light, and even the sense of touch. Floating in these specialized pods can have profound effects on both mental and physical health, making it a perfect practice for retirees seeking inner peace, pain relief, and overall well-being.

I discovered the magic of sensory deprivation a few years ago, and it quickly became a vital part of my self-care routine. There's a sensory deprivation center where I live, and after just one session, I was hooked. I remember stepping out of the pod feeling like a new person—completely refreshed, with a clear mind and relaxed body. I felt as though I'd hit a reset button. Needless to say, I immediately purchased a membership and now make it a priority to float twice a month. Each session feels like a retreat—a space where I can unwind and let go of the stresses of everyday life. It's become a sanctuary for me, a place where both my body and mind can truly rest.

The benefits of sensory deprivation floats are well-documented. Physically, the absence of gravity allows your muscles and joints to fully relax, which can be especially beneficial for those dealing with arthritis, chronic pain, or tension. The magnesium in the Epsom salts also helps soothe sore muscles and reduce inflammation. Mentally, sensory deprivation offers a unique opportunity to quiet the mind, which can reduce stress and anxiety, and promote a deeper sense of relaxation. Studies have shown that regular float sessions can help lower cortisol levels, improve sleep quality, and even spark creativity by providing a space for uninterrupted thought.

Getting started with sensory deprivation floating is as easy as finding a wellness center or spa that offers float therapy. These facilities often provide private float pods or rooms where you can enjoy a session in complete solitude. The typical float lasts between 60 and 90 minutes, although shorter or longer sessions are available depending on personal preference. Before entering the float pod, take a quick shower and put on earplugs to block out any lingering noise. Once inside the pod, the temperature of the water and air is set to match your body's temperature, creating a seamless transition between the two and enhancing the sensation of weightlessness.

As with any new wellness practice, it's important to consult with your doctor before trying sensory deprivation floats, especially if you have any health concerns like claustrophobia, low blood pressure, or skin sensitivities to salt. The ideal water temperature for floatation therapy is typically set between 93.5°F and 96°F (34°C to 35.5°C), which matches skin temperature, allowing for the perfect float experience. Start with shorter sessions of around 30 to 45 minutes, gradually increasing to the standard 60-90 minute float as your body becomes accustomed to the practice.

Floating in sensory deprivation pods can be a refreshing addition to your wellness journey, offering a unique blend of physical relief and mental clarity. If you're interested in floating but don't have a local center, keep in mind that this practice has become increasingly popular worldwide, and you can plan to visit a floating center during your travels. See the **Resources Chapter** for a list of some floating centers worldwide.

3.5 Fitness at Home: Online Classes and Resources

If you prefer to stay active without leaving the comfort of your home, online workout classes are perfect for you. Selecting appropriate workouts is crucial. **Yoga** is an excellent choice for flexibility and relaxation, while **chair yoga** offers a gentler alternative for those with mobility issues. If you're looking for something more dynamic, **Pilates** strengthens core muscles and improves posture. **Tabata** is a high-intensity interval training that can be adapted to your fitness level, and **low-impact aerobics** keeps the heart pumping without too much strain. **Strength training** with light dumbbells can help maintain muscle mass and bone density, which is super important as we age.

The beauty of modern technology is that you have countless online platforms at your fingertips. Websites like **YouTube** offer free classes on anything from yoga to dance workouts. Platforms such as **Peloton** and **Daily Burn** provide live classes and on-demand videos, allowing you to follow along in real-time or at your convenience. These platforms often include progress tracking features, so you can see how much you've improved over time. Apps like **Apple Fitness Plus, MyFitnessPal, BetterMe, and FitOn** also offer curated workout plans tailored to your goals and fitness levels, making it easier than ever to stay on track.

Creating a home gym doesn't require a lot of space or a large investment. Start with minimal equipment like resistance bands, which are versatile and easy to store. A yoga mat and a sturdy chair (for chair yoga) are also great additions. You can use dumbbells of various weights for a wide range of exercises. The key is to have your equipment easily accessible so that you're more likely to use it regularly.

Safety is just as important when working out at home as in the gym. Always begin with a proper warm-up to prepare your muscles and joints. Understand your body's limits and avoid pushing yourself too hard. Start slow and gradually increase the intensity of your workouts. If you're unsure about a specific exercise or routine, seek professional advice. Personal trainers can offer virtual consultations to ensure you're performing exercises correctly, minimizing the risk of injury.

3.6 Gardening for Fitness, Mindfulness, and Growth

Stepping into my garden with the morning dew on the leaves and the fresh scent of the earth all around is my perfect moment of pure connection with nature. But gardening is not just a pleasant pastime; it's a full-body workout wrapped in nature's embrace. There are a few options to start a senior-friendly garden. **Raised beds** are very popular and for a good reason—they bring the soil to you, so no more bending and stooping. **Container gardening** is another fantastic option, allowing you to grow plants on patios or balconies with minimal effort. These methods make gardening accessible and enjoyable, no matter your physical condition.

The physical activities involved in gardening are deceptively beneficial. Digging, planting, weeding, and harvesting might seem like simple tasks, but they engage multiple muscle groups and improve flexibility and strength. Each movement, from pushing a wheelbarrow to pulling out weeds, contributes to overall fitness. It's like hitting the gym but with the added bonus of fresh air and sunshine. Plus, the satisfaction of seeing your hard work bloom into beautiful flowers or tasty vegetables is a reward in itself.

That said, safety is key when gardening, especially for us, seniors. Always take precautions to prevent overexertion or injury. First, protect yourself from the sun by wearing a wide-brimmed hat, sunglasses, and sunscreen with at least SPF 30, especially during midday hours when the sun's rays are strongest. Stay hydrated, as gardening is physically demanding, especially on hot days. Take regular breaks in the shade to avoid heat exhaustion.

When using tools, opt for ergonomically designed tools with padded grips to minimize strain on your hands and wrists. Wearing gloves can protect your skin from thorns, blisters, or insect bites. Bend from your knees, not your back, when lifting heavy items like bags of soil or plants, and use a kneeling pad or gardening stool to reduce pressure on your knees during tasks that require crouching. Consider installing a drip irrigation system to reduce the need for heavy watering cans or hoses.

Incorporating mindfulness into your gardening practice can elevate this activity from a hobby to a form of therapy. Focus on the sensory experiences—the texture of the soil, the vibrant colors of the flowers, and the songs of the birds. These moments of mindfulness help you stay present and grounded, reducing stress and enhancing emotional well-being. Gardening becomes more than just a task; it's an opportunity to connect deeply with nature and find peace in the process.

Community gardening offers another layer of benefits. Participating in a community garden can increase social interaction, allowing you to share gardening responsibilities and learn from others. It's a collaborative effort that fosters a sense of belonging and mutual support. You don't need a space at home to enjoy the fruits of your labor. Community gardens provide plots for you to cultivate your plants, and the shared environment creates opportunities for friendships and community building.

3.7 Tai Chi and Qigong: Gentle Movements for Strength and Balance

Tai Chi and Qigong are ancient Chinese practices where you move like water, flowing smoothly from one pose to another. Originating centuries ago, Tai Chi is a martial art focused on slow, deliberate movements, while Qigong combines breathing techniques with gentle motions. Both are rooted in the principles of balance, flexibility, and inner peace, making them beneficial for seniors. The deliberate pace of Tai Chi and Qigong helps improve balance and strength without the strain of high-impact exercises. Plus, the focus on mindful movement can enhance mental clarity and reduce stress.

Embarking on the journey of Tai Chi and Qigong offers a unique blend of physical and mental enrichment. As you delve into the basics, focusing on your alignment and breath, you'll gradually see your flexibility and strength enhance. What's important about these practices is their versatility; they can be adapted for standing or seated positions. Their slow, graceful motions serve as a meditative exercise, nurturing both your body and mind.

Finding classes and resources tailored to seniors can enhance your learning experience. Look for local community centers or senior centers that offer Tai Chi and Qigong classes. Many instructors specialize in teaching older adults, ensuring the movements are safe and effective. Online resources, such as instructional videos, video courses on **Udemy**, and virtual classes, can also be valuable. **YouTube** or dedicated Tai Chi platforms like **Taichiapp.com** provide step-by-step guides you can follow at your own pace. Choose instructors with experience in senior fitness to ensure you're getting the most appropriate and beneficial instruction.

Integrating Tai Chi and Qigong into your daily routine can bring lasting benefits. Start your morning with a short session to set a calm and focused tone for the day. Incorporate the practices into your evening routine to unwind and prepare for a restful night. Regular practice can help maintain your physical health and enhance mental tranquility. Consider joining a local group for regular sessions, which can provide a sense of community and additional motivation. The gentle, rhythmic movements can become a cherished part of your daily life, supporting you on your retirement journey.

3.8 Paddling to Health: Kayaking, Canoeing, and Paddleboarding

Kayaking, canoeing, and paddleboarding are fantastic ways to stay fit, connect with nature, and find peace of mind, all while engaging in a low-impact, full-body workout. These activities are perfect for retirees looking to explore new adventures while promoting physical and mental well-being. They provide excellent cardiovascular exercise without putting undue strain on your joints. They engage your core, arms, and back muscles, improving balance and flexibility while also building upper body strength. For those dealing with arthritis or joint pain, paddling can offer a gentle yet effective way to stay active while reducing the impact on knees and hips compared to land-based exercises. Beyond the physical benefits, spending time on the water can enhance mental well-being. The fluid, repetitive motions involved in paddling make these activities a calming form of exercise, reducing stress as you glide across calm lakes, rivers, or coastal waters. Studies have shown that being near or on water can lower stress levels, improve mood, and promote a sense of calm. Whether you're navigating a quiet river in a kayak, paddling across a glassy lake on a stand-up paddleboard (SUP), or exploring winding waterways in a canoe, these activities offer a unique opportunity to escape the hustle and bustle of everyday life and reconnect with nature.

Getting started with paddling is both accessible and affordable, making it a perfect hobby for retirees looking to enjoy the outdoors. You don't need a lot of experience or expensive gear to begin; starting with a leisurely kayak or canoe trip on a calm lake or river is a great way to ease into the sport. For beginners, however, it's highly recommended to take a safety course offered by kayak and canoe clubs. These courses teach essential skills such as paddling techniques, safety measures, and handling various water conditions, ensuring your time on the water is enjoyable and worry-free. Many outdoor centers and national parks also offer rentals and guided tours, allowing you to explore new areas with confidence while learning from experienced instructors.

For those seeking a bit more adventure, paddleboarding (SUP) is a fantastic way to challenge your balance and engage your core. While it may look difficult at first, paddleboarding is surprisingly easy to pick up with a bit of practice. Beginners can start by kneeling on the board before standing up, giving you time to get comfortable with the movements.

Kayaking, canoeing, and paddleboarding can also be tailored to your fitness level. If you're looking for a more challenging workout, choose a faster-paced paddle along a coastal route or a river with gentle currents. If relaxation is your goal, a slow-paced paddle across a peaceful lake at sunset offers the perfect blend of exercise and tranquility.

Safety is paramount when paddling. Always check the weather forecast before heading out and avoid paddling in rough conditions if you're not experienced. Stick to calm waters when you're starting and paddle with a buddy or join a group. Most importantly, take your time and enjoy the journey—paddling is as much about the peaceful moments as it is about the physical activity. If you don't have local waterways, consider making paddling part of your next vacation. Many popular travel destinations now offer kayak or paddleboard rentals, making it easy to explore new areas by water, even while traveling.

I still remember my first time in a kayak—gently gliding across a quiet lake, the sounds of nature all around me, and a deep sense of peace settling in as I moved with the water. What began as a weekend adventure quickly turned into a regular hobby. Living on Vancouver Island, my husband and I make it a point to explore the island's many lakes and rivers. Kayaking has become our way of staying fit while embracing the natural beauty of the island, and every paddle through these picturesque waters brings us closer to the outdoor paradise we're lucky to call home.

3.9 Nordic Walking: A Whole-Body Approach to Staying Active

Nordic walking offers a powerful blend of physical and mental health benefits that can transform your retirement years. By using specially designed poles, this activity engages not only your legs but your upper body and core, providing a full-body workout. It improves cardiovascular health, strengthens muscles, and enhances mood, all while enjoying time spent outdoors. Nordic walking groups and clubs offer both physical exercise and the camaraderie of like-minded individuals. Whether it's a leisurely walk through a local park or a more challenging trail, Nordic walking caters to various fitness levels, ensuring everyone can participate and experience the rewards.

The term "Nordic walking" originates from Finland, where it was developed as a form of off-season training for cross-country skiers in the early 20th century. Skiers needed a way to maintain their fitness levels during the snow-free months, and they discovered that walking with poles, mimicking the movement of cross-country skiing, provided an excellent cardiovascular and full-body workout. Over time, this training method became popular outside the skiing community, evolving into what we now know as Nordic walking.

Finding the right group to walk with can make the experience even more enjoyable. Local community centers, senior groups, or online platforms like **Meetup.com** are great resources for finding Nordic walking clubs that match your fitness level and interests. Some clubs focus on easygoing walks, perfect for those who prefer a relaxed pace and enjoy chatting along the way. Others might cater to more adventurous walkers, offering routes with gentle inclines or longer distances that push your limits. Joining a club not only provides motivation but also introduces you to new trails and destinations you might not have discovered on your own. Plus, the social aspect adds a layer of fun and accountability, making it easier to stay committed to a regular walking routine.

Having the right equipment is key to getting the most out of your Nordic walking experience. First, you'll need a quality pair of Nordic walking poles, which are designed to provide support and engage your upper body. Make sure they are adjustable for your height and have comfortable grips. Appropriate footwear is also essential—sturdy, comfortable shoes with good grip and support will make your walks more enjoyable and help prevent injury. Dressing in layers is important and hydration is just as crucial in Nordic walking as it is in hiking. A small backpack can carry your essentials, including snacks, water, a first-aid kit, and your phone.

Whether you're walking in a local park or on a forest trail, safety and etiquette ensure everyone enjoys the experience. Stick to marked trails to protect the environment and avoid getting lost, and always let someone know your route and estimated return time, especially if walking alone. The "Leave No Trace" principle is vital—pack out all trash, respect wildlife, and leave natural areas as you found them. Proper etiquette on shared trails includes yielding to other hikers and bikers, staying to the right, and maintaining control of your poles to avoid obstructing others. Carry a whistle or signaling device for emergencies, and always be mindful of your surroundings, especially in more remote areas.

Nordic walking is an accessible and effective way to stay active while exploring the great outdoors. It provides a low-impact workout that's gentle on the joints yet highly effective for building strength and improving cardiovascular health. For retirees, it offers the perfect balance between fitness, fun, and social interaction, helping you stay engaged with your community and the natural world. With the right gear, a little preparation, and a supportive walking group, Nordic walking can become a rewarding part of your routine, giving you both physical and emotional benefits.

3.10 Leisurely Rides: Scenic Biking Routes for Casual Cyclists

The gentle breeze against your skin as you cycle down a charming path, sunlight filtering through the leaves, creating patterns of light and shadow. That's the beauty of casual cycling. Choosing the right bicycle can make this vision a reality. For older adults, comfort and safety are paramount. A step-through frame, which allows you to easily mount and dismount, can be very helpful. Ergonomic handlebars reduce strain on your wrists, and a cushioned saddle ensures you won't be wincing in pain after a long ride. Consider bikes with wider tires for stability and shock absorption, and don't forget to look for models with gears that can handle various terrains without requiring Herculean effort. E-bikes are also worth considering—they provide an extra boost on tough inclines or longer rides, making cycling more accessible and enjoyable. My husband, who's an avid cyclist, switched to an e-bike a few years ago and finds it a great workout that allows him to explore so much more without overexertion.

Now that you've got the perfect bike, where should you ride? Scenic routes can turn a simple bike ride into a breathtaking adventure. You don't even need to travel far—many cities and towns have beautiful bike paths waiting to be explored. Local routes can be just as stunning and provide a great way to discover the hidden gems in your own backyard. For example, in Victoria, British Columbia, where we live, the **Galloping Goose Trail** is a perfect spot for cyclists of all levels. Stretching over 34 miles, it winds through urban landscapes, forests, and waterfront areas, offering a peaceful escape while staying close to home. Whether you want a quick ride or a long day on the trail, it's a fantastic way to experience the beauty of Vancouver Island without having to venture too far.

The **Confederation Trail** on Prince Edward Island is a must, with over 270 miles of flat, easy riding through charming villages and lush landscapes. The **Icefields Parkway** in Alberta offers a more challenging ride with breathtaking views of the Rockies, glaciers, and turquoise lakes.

For those in the USA, in the East, the **Virginia Creeper Trail** offers a gentle, 34-mile ride through forests and farmlands. In the Midwest, the **Katy Trail** in Missouri provides 240 miles of scenic beauty, winding through small towns and along the Missouri River. On the West Coast, the **Monterey Bay Coastal Recreation Trail** offers stunning views of the ocean and plenty of spots to stop and enjoy the scenery.

Over in Europe, the **Danube Cycle Path** is one of the continent's most popular routes, stretching from Germany to Hungary along the beautiful Danube River. In France, the **Loire Valley** offers a picturesque ride through vineyards, historic castles, and quaint villages. These scenic paths offer a stunning journey that connects with nature and nourishes the soul. Whether you're exploring local trails or traveling to renowned routes across the globe, there's always a scenic ride waiting for you.

Joining local cycling clubs can enhance your biking experience. These clubs often organize regular rides, providing a fantastic opportunity to meet new people and stay motivated. Whether you're a newbie or a seasoned cyclist, there's likely a group that matches your pace and interests. Participating in group rides adds a social element to your fitness routine, turning solitary exercise into a shared adventure. The camaraderie and friendly competition can make each ride more enjoyable and rewarding.

Preparation and safety should never be an afterthought. Always wear a well-fitted helmet; it's the simplest way to protect yourself. Visibility gear, like reflective vests and lights, ensures that you're seen by motorists, especially in low-light conditions. Before each ride, give your bike a quick once-over—check the brakes, tires, and chain to ensure everything is in working order. Carry a small toolkit for minor repairs and a first-aid kit for any unexpected scrapes. Hydration is key, so bring along an extra water bottle. With these precautions, you can pedal away with peace of mind, ready to soak in the beauty and freedom that scenic biking offers.

3.11 Cross-Country Skiing: A Workout for Winter Wellness

Cross-country skiing is an excellent way to stay active and embrace the beauty of winter landscapes. Unlike downhill skiing, cross-country skiing is a low-impact, full-body workout that is gentle on the joints while effectively engaging muscles across your entire body. This activity improves cardiovascular health, boosts endurance, and strengthens major muscle groups like your core, arms, and legs. Skiing at your own pace also allows you to adjust the intensity, making it accessible to a wide range of fitness levels.

If you're new to cross-country skiing, start by selecting the right equipment. You'll need a set of lightweight skis, poles, and boots specifically designed for this type of skiing. Skis should be matched to your height, weight, and skill level to ensure smooth movement across the snow. It's a good idea to rent equipment from a local ski shop before committing to a purchase, especially as you're learning the basics.

Once you have the gear, look for beginner-friendly trails with groomed tracks that make it easier to glide and maintain balance. Local parks, nature reserves, and ski resorts often have trails designated for cross-country skiing. Most locations will offer trails rated by difficulty, so start with flat or gently rolling terrain until you feel comfortable with your movements. Taking a lesson from a local instructor or joining a cross-country skiing club can also help you quickly learn proper techniques like how to glide efficiently, use your poles for momentum, and climb small hills.

It's essential to take a few precautions to ensure a safe and enjoyable experience. Because this activity can be physically demanding, always warm up with light stretching before hitting the trails. Pay attention to your body's signals, and pace yourself—especially if you're just starting or returning to skiing after a long break. Hydration is key even in colder weather, so bring water or a sports drink with you. It's also important to protect yourself from the elements. Dress in layers so you can adjust your warmth as you build up a sweat on the trails. A moisture-wicking base layer, an insulating mid-layer, and a waterproof outer layer will help keep you dry and comfortable throughout your adventure. Sunscreen is a must, as UV rays can reflect off the snow, and sunglasses will shield your eyes from glare. Make sure you have a map of the trails or use a GPS app, particularly if you're skiing in a remote area.

One of the best parts of cross-country skiing is exploring beautiful winter trails at your own pace. Many ski resorts and parks across the **USA, Canada, and Europe** offer designated cross-country skiing routes, ranging from easy loops to more challenging paths through forests and open fields. In the USA, popular spots include the groomed trails at **Methow Valley in Washington** and **Devil's Thumb Ranch in Colorado**, where skiers can glide along picturesque snow-covered landscapes. Canada also offers spectacular cross-country skiing opportunities, with **Banff National Park** and **Gatineau Park near Ottawa** providing stunning views of snow-capped mountains and frozen lakes.

For those looking to venture further, Europe boasts incredible cross-country skiing destinations as well. In **Norway**, the trails around **Lillehammer and Sjusjøen** offer a mix of tranquil forest routes and open mountain landscapes, perfect for all skill levels. **Finland's Lapland region,** especially around **Ylläs and Levi**, provides a magical experience with trails winding through snow-covered forests and past frozen lakes, often illuminated by the Northern Lights. **Austria's Seefeld** is another top destination, known for its world-class cross-country skiing facilities set against the backdrop of the Austrian Alps. **Sweden's Dalarna region**, home to the famous Vasaloppet race, offers extensive trail networks and breathtaking scenery for skiers looking to challenge themselves or enjoy a peaceful winter escape.

For a more leisurely experience, consider skiing on flat terrain at local golf courses or community parks, where you can take in the beauty of nature without the strain of hilly trails. Many parks and resorts offer rentals and lessons, making it easy to enjoy cross-country skiing with no need to invest in equipment right away.

3.12 Cooking for Health: Fun Workshops and Classes

Cooking is an art form that can significantly enhance your health as you advance in age. Learning healthy cooking techniques can revolutionize your diet and overall well-being. For instance, steaming a vibrant array of vegetables not only preserves their nutrients but also ensures your meal is light and flavorful. Opting to grill a piece of fish and season it with herbs and spices yields a dish that's both healthy and delicious. Adding herbs and spices like turmeric, ginger, and garlic infuses your meals with flavor while bringing many health benefits—such as anti-inflammatory properties and antioxidant support—transforming every dish into a mini wellness feast. These methods not only elevate the taste of your food but also bolster your health, providing both nutrition and enjoyment in every bite.

Understanding the specific nutritional needs of seniors is vital, as your body requires different nutrients with age. For example, increasing fiber intake, lowering cholesterol, and incorporating more vitamins and minerals are crucial for maintaining a healthy body and mind. Learning how to prepare meals that meet these needs can be transformative. Many cooking classes and resources focus specifically on seniors, helping you prepare recipes that are high in fiber, packed with vitamins, and low in cholesterol. Think of it as acquiring a culinary education tailored to your body's evolving requirements. Resources like **America's Test Kitchen Online Cooking School** and **Rouxbe** provide in-depth cooking lessons, including those focused on nutrition and healthy eating, guiding you step-by-step through creating meals that nourish both body and soul.

Cooking can also be a communal affair. Social cooking events turn the kitchen into a dynamic social space. In a cooking workshop, the experience goes beyond just learning a new recipe—it's about laughter, shared stories, and forging new friendships. These gatherings foster a sense of community, blending education with social interaction. Whether you're rolling dough alongside someone or debating the ideal mix of herbs, the connections formed are as enriching as the cuisine. **Meetup.com** is a great online resource for finding local cooking classes and events where you can bond with like-minded people while sharpening your culinary skills. Many local community centers, culinary institutes, and even supermarkets offer classes focused on both healthy cooking techniques and nutrition. For those who prefer to learn at their own pace, digital platforms like **MasterClass** and **Udemy** offer cooking courses taught by renowned chefs, allowing you to hone your skills from the comfort of home. You can explore a wide variety of cooking styles and cuisines, with lessons ranging from basic techniques to gourmet meals. With these resources at your fingertips, you're never too far from your next culinary adventure, whether you're cooking for health, for fun, or for community connection.

3.13 Relax, Renew, Rebalance: Spa and Hot Springs Escapes

Sinking into a warm, bubbling hot tub, the stresses of daily life melt away as you take in the serene surroundings. Spa retreats offer more than just a day of pampering; they provide a rejuvenating experience that can significantly improve your health and well-being. These retreats combine relaxation with health benefits, such as reducing stress, alleviating chronic pain, and enhancing your general sense of well-being through therapies like massages, hydrotherapy, and yoga. The word "spa" itself originates from the Belgian town of Spa, which became famous for its mineral-rich thermal springs as early as the 14th century. The healing properties of its waters attracted visitors from across Europe, and soon the term "spa" became synonymous with places offering water-based therapies. Today, spas worldwide incorporate a variety of treatments designed to relax the body and mind, from ancient mineral baths to modern luxury retreats.

Picture yourself enjoying a massage that loosens tight muscles or a hydrotherapy session that soothes arthritis pain, leaving you feeling refreshed and revitalized. There are plenty of spa retreats worldwide that offer a range of therapeutic treatments tailored to individual wellness needs. Please refer to the **Resources Chapter** for a list of renowned Spa Retreats.

Your luxurious spa experience doesn't have to be expensive. You don't need to travel far or break the bank to enjoy the benefits of a spa day. In fact, nearly every town has local spas, and many are located in hotels or wellness centers. Many local spas offer affordable services, especially if you take advantage of senior discounts or special packages designed for specific days like Mother's Day, Valentine's Day, or even "spa week" promotions that offer reduced rates. Hotel spas often have day passes that allow you to enjoy their facilities without booking an overnight stay. Some gyms and community centers even offer spa services like massages, facials, and saunas at much lower rates than high-end resorts. Planning ahead and taking advantage of these deals can allow you to pamper yourself regularly, without the high price tag of a luxury resort. Whether you're looking for a simple massage or a more comprehensive wellness package, there's likely an affordable option nearby that fits your needs.

One particularly powerful spa experience comes from **hot springs**. Bathing in natural hot springs has been practiced for centuries, revered for its therapeutic benefits. The warm waters naturally raise your body temperature, dilating blood vessels and improving circulation. This increased blood flow helps deliver oxygen and nutrients to tissues more efficiently, promoting healing and pain relief for conditions like arthritis and fibromyalgia. The buoyancy of the water also relieves pressure on joints, making it easier to move and stretch without discomfort.

Meanwhile, the minerals in the water are absorbed through the skin, with elements like sulfur helping with skin conditions, calcium aiding in bone health, and magnesium easing muscle pain.

The calming environment of natural hot springs, often surrounded by stunning landscapes, also promotes mental well-being. The serene settings—whether nestled in the mountains, by a forest, or overlooking a coastal view—offer a break from the chaos of daily life, providing a moment of tranquility that can soothe the mind. Please refer to the **Resources Chapter** for a list of Hot Springs Retreats.

Preparing for your spa experience involves a bit of planning to maximize your comfort and enjoyment. Pack light, comfortable clothing, a swimsuit, and any personal items that make you feel at home. Communicate any specific health concerns to the staff before you arrive, so they can tailor treatments to your needs. Expect a mix of relaxation and gentle activity, and approach the experience with an open mind, ready to embrace the therapeutic benefits. Knowing what to expect can help you relax and fully immerse yourself in the experience.

Taking part in wellness programs offered by spa retreats can enhance the benefits of your stay. Many retreats include fitness classes, nutritional workshops, and mindfulness sessions as part of their programs. These activities provide a holistic approach to wellness, addressing both physical and mental health. Engaging in these programs can help you learn new skills and habits to take home, ensuring that the benefits of your spa retreat extend well beyond your stay.

By exploring spa and hot spring retreats, you're investing not just in your relaxation but in your overall well-being. Whether it's the soothing warmth of a natural hot spring or the calming energy of a luxurious spa, these experiences provide long-lasting physical and mental benefits that will enrich your retirement.

Taking care of your body and mind is essential for living your best life in retirement. But staying healthy is just one part of this exciting new chapter. Now that you're feeling rejuvenated, it's time to broaden your horizons and embrace all the world has to offer. Whether it's exploring new cultures or diving into global adventures, the next chapter will open doors to exciting travel opportunities, new experiences, and ways to engage with the world around you. Let's dive in and discover how your next adventure could be just a plane ride—or a short drive—away.

4

The World at Your Fingertips: Senior-Friendly Destinations, Budgets, and Beyond

The world is more accessible than ever, and retirement opens up new possibilities for exploring it at your own pace. Are you dreaming of visiting famous historic destinations? Embarking on a group travel adventure? Enjoying the freedom of solo travel? Whatever it is, there's something for every kind of traveler. Even if you have physical limitations, the travel industry has adapted to make the globe more accessible than ever before. In this chapter, we'll dive into the best destinations, tips for group and solo travel, and practical advice for navigating the world with physical limitations, ensuring your adventures are safe, enjoyable, and, of course, unforgettable.

4.1 The Best Senior-Friendly Travel Destinations Worldwide

When selecting a destination for your next adventure, a few key considerations can make all the difference in ensuring a smooth and enjoyable trip. Start by thinking about healthcare facilities—having access to quality medical care offers peace of mind, particularly when traveling far from home. It's also important to assess the accessibility of the destination. Opt for places with well-maintained sidewalks, ramps, and accessible public transportation that cater to mobility needs, allowing you to explore comfortably and confidently.

Another crucial factor is senior-friendly transportation. Look for destinations with efficient systems, such as buses with low floors or areas where taxis are readily available. This will make getting around much easier and stress-free.

To streamline your planning, keep a simple checklist in mind: reliable healthcare, easy accessibility, safe and efficient transportation, and, of course, plenty of attractions that inspire your curiosity. With these essentials covered, you can focus on the excitement of your journey, knowing that both comfort and adventure await you at every turn.

Now, let's dive into some of the top destinations that cater specifically to seniors, offering a blend of accessibility, culture, and ease of exploration. **Florence, Italy**, with its rich art scene and relatively flat terrain, is ideal for leisurely strolls through centuries of history. Explore iconic sites like the Uffizi Gallery and the Duomo without worrying about steep climbs. The city's compact layout means that many of its best attractions are within walking distance, and accessible transport options ensure a smooth visit.

Kyoto, Japan, is another perfect destination for those seeking serenity combined with accessibility. Its stunning temples and zen gardens, such as the Golden Pavilion and Fushimi Inari Shrine, offer peaceful escapes. The city's efficient public transport, including buses and subways with senior-friendly options, ensures you can move around with ease.

In **Barcelona, Spain**, you can enjoy world-class architecture with Gaudi's masterpieces, like the Sagrada Familia and Park Güell, and many senior discounts at major attractions. The city's wide boulevards, accessible public transportation, and plentiful benches in parks and along promenades make it a senior-friendly spot for exploring. Whether you're strolling down Las Ramblas or savoring tapas at a local café, Barcelona offers something for every taste, all with comfort in mind.

Vienna, Austria, is renowned for its grandeur and senior-friendly amenities. From the majestic Schönbrunn Palace to its opera houses, the city offers accessible transportation and discounted tickets for seniors at many of its iconic attractions. With its flat streets and easy access to parks and cafes, Vienna is ideal for leisurely exploring its rich heritage.

For those looking for hidden gems, **Ljubljana, Slovenia**, is a fantastic option. This small, compact city boasts a charming old town where you can easily explore its picturesque streets and bridges. Ljubljana also stands out for its excellent health facilities and affordable, accessible public transportation, making it a secure and tranquil place for senior travelers to enjoy.

For a fairy-tale vibe, head to **Bruges, Belgium**, a small, easily navigable city known for its winding canals and stunning medieval architecture. Whether you're taking a boat ride through the canals or wandering its picturesque streets, Bruges offers a relaxed pace perfect for senior travelers.

In **Stockholm, Sweden**, an efficient transport system makes it easy to get around, with many of the city's museums, parks, and attractions offering senior discounts. The city's blend of urban life and easy access to nature creates a perfect balance, with plenty of quiet spots to relax by the water or take a leisurely boat tour through its archipelago.

For those seeking bike-friendly cities, **Amsterdam and Copenhagen** offer extensive cycling paths, senior-friendly public transport, and easy access to cultural hotspots. With flat terrain and beautiful canals, these cities offer a scenic and enjoyable way to explore on two wheels.

Closer to home, **Charleston, South Carolina**, offers a slice of Southern charm with its cobblestone streets, historic plantations, and antebellum mansions. Charleston is known for its walkable downtown area and senior-friendly guided tours that bring history to life. Explore its gardens or indulge in Lowcountry cuisine, as Charleston delivers a warm and welcoming experience with ease of movement and plenty of relaxing spots to take a break.

In Canada, **Banff**, located in the heart of the Rocky Mountains, provides a stunning backdrop of snow-capped peaks and crystal-clear lakes. Banff offers both adventure and tranquility for nature lovers: take in the views from the Banff Gondola or enjoy a quiet hike on one of the area's many accessible trails. Senior discounts on park fees and accessible amenities in its hotels and restaurants make Banff an excellent choice for a stress-free retreat.

If you're looking for a city steeped in history, **Quebec City, Canada,** delivers cobblestone streets, historic architecture, and charming shops, all within a compact, walkable area. Senior discounts on public transport and at some of the city's main attractions make exploring Old Quebec a hassle-free experience. For added convenience and a touch of adventure, take the city's funicular, which connects the upper and lower parts of Old Quebec. This scenic ride offers easy access to different areas of the city and is an attraction in itself, giving you a unique view of the historic landscape as you travel between the two levels.

Across the globe in **Sydney, Australia**, seniors can enjoy scenic harbor views, world-class museums, and famous landmarks like the Sydney

Opera House and Bondi Beach. The city's efficient public transport includes senior discounts, and many attractions are easily accessible. For those who enjoy the outdoors, the Botanical Gardens offer serene paths perfect for a relaxed walk by the water.

If a laid-back atmosphere with scenic harbor views is more your style, consider **Wellington, New Zealand**. With its excellent public transportation, waterfront promenades, and access to nature trails, Wellington provides a calm yet vibrant experience. Be sure to explore its art galleries and enjoy its famous coffee culture.

As you plan your travels, keep in mind that some developing nations might not have the same level of infrastructure for senior travelers. Doing research is essential, especially when it comes to accessibility, healthcare options, and reliable transportation. Always check if attractions offer senior discounts, guided tours in your language, and accessible facilities like ramps and elevators to ensure a smooth and enjoyable journey. With the right preparation, the world truly becomes an open invitation to explore at your own pace.

4.2 The Best Travel Times for an Unforgettable Experience

The timing of your trip can be the difference between a perfect getaway and a frustrating experience. One of the best ways to ensure smooth travel is to avoid extreme weather and peak tourist crowds by opting for shoulder seasons—the periods just before or after the high season in many destinations. Spring and fall typically offer mild weather, fewer tourists, and often lower prices, giving you the best of both worlds: pleasant conditions and a more relaxed atmosphere.

Take **Greece** as an example. Visiting in May means you'll experience comfortable temperatures ideal for exploring ancient ruins, wandering through charming villages, and enjoying the blooming wildflowers that blanket the countryside. Plus, you'll miss the sweltering heat and bustling crowds of summer, allowing for a more peaceful exploration of iconic sights like the Acropolis and Santorini cliffs.

For a scenic European trip, consider Italy's **Tuscany** in late September, when the weather is still warm but the summer crowds have thinned out. This is especially important because in August, Italy celebrates **Ferragosto**, a national holiday that marks the peak of summer. During this time, many Italians take extended vacations, and businesses in popular tourist areas may be closed. Crowds flock to the beaches and cities, making travel more hectic and accommodations harder to find. By late September, however, the bustle of Ferragosto has passed, and you can enjoy Tuscany's rolling hills, charming villages, and world-renowned vineyards in a more relaxed and peaceful setting.

Japan's breathtaking cherry blossom season in April is a beautiful time to visit. As delicate pink flowers blanket parks, temples, and city streets, the country comes alive with celebrations of sakura (cherry blossoms), offering a quintessentially Japanese experience. However, it's also one of the busiest times of the year, so booking early is essential to avoid overcrowded accommodations and ensure you get the best spots for viewing the blossoms.

If autumn colors captivate you, **Canada's Algonquin Park** in September and October is an ideal destination. The vibrant hues of red, orange, and gold set against the park's serene lakes and forests create a mesmerizing landscape, perfect for photographers and nature lovers alike. Hiking trails like the Lookout Trail or the Centennial Ridges Trail provide stunning panoramic views of the autumn foliage. Fall is the prime time for capturing the beauty of this Canadian gem, with fewer crowds than during the summer.

For a quieter Mediterranean escape, consider **Portugal's Algarve region** in October. While summer brings throngs of tourists to its golden beaches, by fall, the crowds have thinned, but the warm sun still graces the coastline. This is the perfect time to explore the Algarve's stunning cliffs, hidden coves, and quaint fishing villages at a more relaxed pace. The region is also home to incredible seafood, so you can enjoy freshly caught fare without the summer rush.

For those seeking a mix of urban sophistication and natural beauty, **Cape Town, South Africa,** in March is an excellent choice. With warm weather and fewer tourists, it's a great time to explore the city's vibrant cultural scene, climb Table Mountain, or visit the nearby Cape Winelands. March also marks the beginning of the whale-watching season along the coast. Head to Hermanus, a short drive from Cape Town, for one of the best shore-based whale-watching experiences in the world.

Always pack layers to accommodate temperature changes and comfortable shoes for all that exploring you'll be doing. Consider bringing a lightweight, waterproof jacket for unexpected rain, and a hat for sun protection. Compression socks can help with long flights, reducing swelling and keeping you comfortable. Don't forget essential medications, and pack an extra supply just in case of travel delays. A small first-aid kit with bandages, pain relievers, and any over-the-counter medications you may need can be a lifesaver. Finally, make sure you have a power adapter if traveling internationally and a photocopy of important documents like your passport. With a bit of planning, each trip can be as comfortable as it is memorable.

4.3 Group Travel: Finding Retirement Travel Clubs

Group travel is an increasingly popular option for retirees, offering many benefits that can make exploring the world both enjoyable and stress-free. One of the main advantages is cost savings—travel clubs often negotiate discounted rates for accommodations, transportation, and excursions, making group travel more affordable. Another significant benefit is enhanced safety. Traveling with a group provides a sense of security, knowing you have others around to navigate unfamiliar places, especially in more remote or challenging destinations. Beyond the practical aspects, group travel offers a unique sense of camaraderie. Shared experiences, from exploring historic landmarks to enjoying meals together, can create lasting friendships. These connections with fellow travelers often make the journey more memorable and enjoyable.

Choosing the right travel club is key to ensuring your trip matches your personal interests and travel style. Many travel clubs cater specifically to retirees, offering everything from luxury cruises to adventure trips and cultural tours. When selecting a travel club, consider the pace of the trips they offer—do they allow for leisurely exploration, or are they packed with a busy itinerary? It's also important to check the destinations they focus on and whether these align with your travel goals. Group size is another consideration; smaller groups often offer a more intimate experience, while larger groups may provide more social opportunities and diverse activities.

Please check the **Resources Chapter** for some reputable group travel companies for retirees.

You can also explore online platforms like **Meetup.com** or **Facebook Groups**, which allow travelers to connect with like-minded individuals and join organized trips or form their own. Websites like **Traveling Alone Together** and **Seniors Travel Club** are additional resources where you can find group travel options and join communities of retirees who love to explore.

Once you've chosen your travel club and destination, preparing for the trip is essential to ensure a smooth experience. Start by gathering all necessary paperwork, such as passports, visas, and travel insurance. Some travel clubs may assist with this process, but it's important to stay organized and double-check everything before you leave. Packing essentials will vary depending on the destination and the type of trip, but it's always a good idea to bring comfortable clothing and shoes for walking, layers for changing weather conditions, and any medications you may need. Consider bringing a small travel journal to jot down experiences along the way. It's also important to set expectations for group travel—while there may be structured activities, it's equally valuable to allow for flexibility and personal time, balancing socializing with relaxation.

4.4 Solo Travel: Exploring the World on Your Own Terms

Traveling solo offers a unique sense of freedom and empowerment, especially in retirement. One of the greatest benefits is complete control over your itinerary—you can explore destinations at your own pace, without having to accommodate the preferences of others. Whether you're an early riser looking to catch the sunrise, or someone who prefers leisurely afternoons exploring museums, solo travel lets you structure your day exactly how you like. Solo travel also encourages personal growth—navigating new environments on your own builds confidence. Plus, it offers a special opportunity for self-reflection and the chance to immerse yourself fully in the experience without distractions.

Another perk of solo travel is the ability to connect with new people. You'll often find that locals and fellow travelers are more likely to engage with you when you're alone, creating opportunities for spontaneous conversations and meaningful connections. Traveling alone doesn't mean you have to be lonely—solo travelers often form bonds with people they meet along the way, sharing meals, stories, and adventures.

Choosing the right destination is essential for ensuring a safe and enjoyable solo travel experience. Safety is a key factor, so look for places known for their traveler-friendly environments and low crime rates. Countries like **Japan, New Zealand,** and **Ireland** are recommended for solo travelers because of their safety, welcoming culture, and well-developed tourist infrastructure.

For those seeking a cultural experience, European cities like **Amsterdam, Vienna,** and **Barcelona** offer easy-to-navigate public transportation, plenty of solo-friendly attractions, and a variety of group tours you can join if you want some company. If nature is more your style, **Costa Rica** is ideal for solo travelers looking for adventure, with its accessible national parks and eco-lodges that provide a sense of community. In the U.S., cities like **Portland, Oregon,** or **Santa Fe, New Mexico**, are known for their solo-traveler-friendly vibe, with walkable streets, cultural experiences, and plenty of safe, social accommodations like boutique hotels or hostels.

Solo travel requires a bit more preparation to ensure a smooth and safe journey. First, always make sure you have adequate travel insurance—this is crucial for covering unexpected events, such as medical issues or cancellations. Having a detailed itinerary that you share with friends or family back home is another way to ensure your safety. It's also a good idea to familiarize yourself with local customs and basic phrases in the local language, especially if you're visiting a non-English-speaking country.

When it comes to packing, it's important to bring items that enhance your sense of safety and comfort. A money belt or hidden pouch can be useful for keeping your valuables secure, and carrying a small first-aid kit ensures you're prepared for any minor emergencies. Solo travelers should download travel apps like **Google Maps, TripIt,** and **Translate**, which can make navigating new destinations easier. Joining solo traveler forums or groups online can provide you with up-to-date travel advice and potential connections with other travelers along the way.

While solo travel is liberating, it's important to stay vigilant, especially when navigating unfamiliar places. Always be aware of your surroundings and trust your instincts. Researching neighborhoods ahead of time can help you avoid unsafe areas. If you're arriving in a new city late at night, consider arranging transportation in advance or staying at accommodations with a 24-hour front desk. Solo travelers should also avoid sharing too much information with strangers, such as your full itinerary or the fact that you're traveling alone.

Using apps like **Airbnb** or staying in hostels with high ratings from fellow solo travelers is a great way to ensure safe accommodations. In larger cities, walking tours and group excursions are excellent ways to explore while enjoying some company. When dining out, treat yourself to a nice restaurant or cafe—it's one of the joys of solo travel! Many solo travelers bring a book, journal, or tablet for company if they prefer quiet time, or strike up a conversation with fellow diners if they're feeling social.

Solo travel doesn't mean you have to go it alone the entire time. There's a thriving community of solo travelers around the world, and joining this community can enhance your experience. Websites and platforms like **Solo Traveler World, Women on the Road,** and **Traveling Alone Together** offer tips, advice, and even meetups for solo travelers. These forums are full of resources and support, with experienced travelers sharing insights on the best destinations, how to stay safe, and how to make the most of traveling alone.

You can also use platforms like **Meetup.com** or **Couchsurfing** to connect with locals or other travelers at your destination. Many cities offer solo traveler meetups, walking tours, or group dinners that provide opportunities to meet new people while maintaining the flexibility of traveling on your own.

Please refer to the Resources Section for a list of companies specializing in solo travel.

4.5 A Comprehensive Guide to Traveling with Physical Limitations

Traveling with disabilities or physical limitations doesn't have to mean limiting your experiences. Whether you're a cane user, a slow walker, or have hearing or vision impairments, some companies specialize in making travel accessible and enjoyable for everyone. For wheelchair users, travelers with complex health issues like dialysis, or those with developmental disabilities, specialized companies like **Easy Access Travel, Planet Abled, Wheel the World, Tapooz Travel**, and **Seable Holidays** provide tailored solutions to ensure a smooth journey. These organizations offer services such as arranging accessible tours, transportation, and accommodations that cater to specific needs. For example, **Easy Access Travel** focuses on cruises and vacations with mobility aids, while **Planet Abled** and **Wheel the World** design inclusive travel experiences across the globe. **Seable Holidays** and **Tapooz Travel** provide unique adventures with support for those who are vision or hearing-impaired. No matter your requirements, these companies are dedicated to helping you see the world comfortably and confidently, ensuring that your travel aspirations are not just possible but fulfilling.

Before packing your bags, a medical check-up is crucial. Your doctor can assess your fitness for travel and update the necessary medications. Discuss travel insurance that covers pre-existing conditions. This isn't just paperwork; it's your safety net. Imagine exploring new places with peace of mind, knowing you're covered if anything unexpected happens.

Choosing the right accommodations and transport options is like picking the perfect pair of shoes for walking—comfort and functionality are key. Look for hotels with wheelchair accessibility, elevators, and proximity to medical facilities. Many places offer accessible rooms with grab bars, roll-in showers, and lower beds. When it comes to getting around, prioritize transport options that cater to your needs, like accessible taxis and buses with low floors. Some destinations even offer specialized services for seniors or those with mobility issues.

Packing for accessibility might sound tedious, but it's the secret sauce to a hassle-free trip. Start with a collapsible cane and a portable seat cushion. Medication organizers ensure you never miss a dose, crucial when you're busy sightseeing. Think about comfort, too. Compression socks can prevent swelling on long flights, and a lightweight, easy-to-carry bag can hold all your essentials. The key is to be prepared without being overburdened.

On-the-ground support services can be your best friend. Before you go, research local healthcare services and accessibility equipment rentals. Many countries offer services that rent out wheelchairs, scooters, or even portable ramps. Knowing where to find these can save you from a lot of stress. Some destinations also have apps or services that connect you with local caregivers or medical professionals. Having a support system in place, ready to help at a moment's notice, is not a luxury, it's a necessity.

4.6 Seeing the World Without Breaking the Bank

Traveling the world doesn't have to be expensive. With a bit of research and flexibility, you can explore incredible destinations without blowing your budget. Whether you're drawn to the historic charm of Europe, the vibrant cultures of Southeast Asia, or the breathtaking landscapes of South America, there are countless budget-friendly options that offer unforgettable experiences. Let's take a look at some of the most affordable yet enriching destinations where you can stretch your travel dollars further.

Eastern Europe: Cities like **Budapest, Hungary, Prague, Czech Republic,** and **Krakow, Poland** offer rich cultural experiences, stunning architecture, and relatively low costs compared to Western Europe. You can explore medieval castles, take river cruises, and enjoy delicious local cuisine at a fraction of the price you'd pay in cities like Paris or Rome. Public transportation is affordable, and many museums and cultural sites offer senior discounts. In **Montenegro**, the coastal town of Kotor, nestled between the Adriatic Sea and rugged mountains, is a **UNESCO World Heritage Site** with affordable accommodations and dining. **Bulgaria** is another hidden gem. **Sofia**, the capital, offers a mix of ancient Roman ruins, Ottoman mosques, and Soviet-era architecture, all at a fraction of the cost of other European capitals. The city of **Plovdiv**, one of the oldest continuously inhabited cities in Europe, offers Roman amphitheaters, art galleries, and charming old town streets to explore.

Southeast Asia: Countries like **Thailand**, **Vietnam**, and **Cambodia** are known for their affordability and breathtaking beauty. In Thailand, you can lounge on white-sand beaches, explore ancient temples, and feast on street food for just a few dollars a day. Vietnam's bustling cities, lush countryside, and UNESCO World Heritage sites like Ha Long Bay offer a blend of adventure and relaxation, with low-cost accommodations and meals. Cambodia's **Angkor Wat** is a must-see, and the cost of living in the country is remarkably low, making it a dream destination for budget-conscious travelers.

South America: Head to **Cusco, Peru** or **Medellín, Colombia,** for vibrant culture, stunning landscapes, and affordable travel experiences. Cusco, the gateway to Machu Picchu, offers fascinating Incan history and beautiful architecture. Meanwhile, Medellín has transformed into a modern, thriving city with great public transportation, beautiful parks, and a lively cultural scene. Both cities offer affordable accommodations, delicious local food, and plenty of free or low-cost activities.

Portugal: **Lisbon** and **Porto** provide a blend of old-world charm and modern vibrancy. With beautiful tile-adorned buildings, scenic waterfronts, and delicious (yet affordable) cuisine, Portugal is an excellent budget-friendly European destination. Public transportation is efficient and cheap, and many attractions offer senior discounts.

Mexico: Beyond the popular resort areas, cities like **Oaxaca** and **Guanajuato** offer rich cultural experiences, local markets, and stunning historical sites at a fraction of the cost. Explore ancient ruins, colorful festivals, and enjoy authentic Mexican cuisine without straining your wallet.

United States: There are many budget-friendly options in the U.S. Cities like **Asheville, North Carolina**, and **Santa Fe, New Mexico**, offer a mix of natural beauty, art, and history. In **Texas**, **San Antonio** offers a scenic River Walk and rich historical sites like the Alamo. **New Orleans, Louisiana** is famous for its unique blend of cultures, vibrant music scene, and delicious Creole and Cajun cuisine. New Orleans offers plenty of free attractions like walking tours of the historic French Quarter, visiting St. Louis Cathedral, or simply soaking up the lively atmosphere on Bourbon Street. **Memphis, Tennessee, is k**nown for its role in American music history. Memphis offers budget-friendly experiences like visiting Beale Street for live blues performances, exploring Sun Studio, and paying respects at the National Civil Rights Museum. **Kansas City, Missouri,** famous for its barbecue and jazz scene, also boasts free attractions like the Nelson-Atkins Museum of

Art and City Market. The city's affordable accommodations and public transportation make it an excellent choice for budget-conscious travelers. **St. Augustine, Florida** is the nation's oldest city; it offers plenty of affordable history and charm. Stroll through the cobblestone streets, explore Castillo de San Marcos, and visit the Fountain of Youth Archaeological Park without breaking the bank. **Salt Lake City, Utah,** is a gateway to the great outdoors with stunning views of the surrounding mountains, close to national parks Arches and Zion. The city itself has budget-friendly attractions like Temple Square and free outdoor concerts in the summer. **Albuquerque, New Mexico,** known for its annual Balloon Fiesta, is an affordable destination year-round. Visit Old Town for its historic charm, explore the Sandia Mountains, or check out the Petroglyph National Monument—all at reasonable prices.

Canada: For a taste of European charm without leaving North America, head to **Montreal**, where you'll find a blend of French and Canadian culture, beautiful old-town streets, and a vibrant art scene. **Halifax, Nova Scotia**, is another excellent choice, offering coastal beauty, maritime history, and affordable prices.

Morocco: For a more exotic yet affordable experience, **Marrakech** offers bustling souks, stunning palaces, and a rich cultural heritage. Accommodations range from budget-friendly riads (traditional guesthouses) to luxury resorts, and exploring the vibrant city streets doesn't cost a thing.

These destinations prove you don't need to spend a fortune to have rich, memorable travel experiences. By opting for less expensive countries and regions, you can immerse yourself in different cultures, enjoy unique attractions, and create lifelong memories—all while staying within your budget. No matter where your retirement adventures take you, the world is full of affordable gems waiting to be explored. Pack your bags and get ready for the journey of a lifetime—without breaking the bank.

5

Epic Journeys of a Lifetime: Unforgettable Travel Experiences

The world is waiting for you. A quaint Parisian café invites you to sip wine with the Eiffel Tower in view. The vibrant markets of Marrakech beckon, rich with the scent of spices and adventure. The ancient stone circles of Avebury draw you in, offering a glimpse into millennia of history. Norway's majestic fjords welcome you to sail through serene waters, where towering cliffs meet the sky. Retirement grants you the freedom to explore at your own pace, without busy schedules. With so many incredible destinations, where will your journey begin? Let's explore how to turn your travel dreams into reality.

5.1 Eco-Tourism: Environmentally Conscious Travel

Eco-tourism is like combining your love for travel with a hearty dose of Mother Nature's TLC. It focuses on sustainable travel practices that minimize your environmental footprint while supporting conservation efforts. As a retiree, you have the chance to contribute to these efforts. Whether it's taking part in a beach cleanup or supporting local eco-friendly businesses, your actions can make a significant impact on preserving these natural wonders for future generations.

Choosing eco-friendly destinations is akin to picking a vacation spot that's as kind to the environment as it is to you. National parks, wildlife reserves, and conservation areas often lead the pack in eco-tourism. Consider the **Galápagos Islands**, where strict regulations protect the unique wildlife, or **Costa Rica's Monteverde Cloud Forest**, renowned for its biodiversity and eco-lodges. **The Serengeti National Park in Tanzania** offers sustainable safaris, while the **Great Barrier Reef in Australia** promotes coral conservation. **Patagonia in Chile** and **Argentina** is a haven for eco-conscious trekkers. For an off-the-beaten-path option, visit **Iceland**, where geothermal energy powers most of the country, and its dramatic landscapes are carefully protected. **Bhutan**, known for its commitment to environmental preservation, limits tourist numbers to protect its natural and cultural heritage. The fjords of **Norway** also offer sustainable tourism, with eco-friendly cruises and a deep respect for preserving the local environment. Other notable mentions include the **Azores in Portugal**, the **Białowieża Forest in Poland,** and **Canada's Banff National Park**. These destinations offer stunning natural beauty and at the same time, prioritize environmental sustainability.

Taking part in conservation activities during your travels adds a layer of purpose to your adventures. You could join a wildlife habitat restoration project, where you help plant native species to restore ecosystems. Guided eco-tours often include educational programs that teach you about local flora and fauna and the importance of conservation. Imagine taking part in a turtle nesting project in **Mexico** or a reforestation effort in the **Amazon.** In **New Zealand,** you might contribute to penguin conservation efforts by maintaining nesting sites. In **Kenya**, some safaris offer opportunities to assist with anti-poaching initiatives or support local wildlife research. In **Iceland**, you could join glacier conservation tours that actively work to monitor and protect fragile ice formations. In the U.S., you could help restore coral reefs in **Florida** or join trail maintenance projects in national parks like **Yosemite** or the **Great Smoky Mountains.** Volunteers can also participate in beach cleanups along the **Pacific Coast** or help protect sea turtles in **North Carolina**. These activities enrich your travel experience and leave a positive mark on the environment. You become a guardian of nature, one trip at a time.

Minimizing your travel footprint is easier than you might think. Start by using public transportation, which reduces carbon emissions compared to private cars. Opt for eco-friendly accommodations—look for places that use renewable energy, reduce waste, and support local communities. Practicing 'Leave No Trace' principles is crucial; always clean up after yourself and avoid disturbing wildlife. Consider packing reusable items like water bottles, shopping bags, cutlery, and travel containers to cut down on single-use plastics. Be mindful of water usage, especially in areas where it's scarce, and try to reduce energy consumption by turning off lights and electronics when not in use. With these simple practices, you can enjoy your travels while keeping the planet green and healthy.

5.2 Voluntourism: Combining Travel with Volunteer Work

Exploring a new country while making a meaningful impact on the local community is what voluntourism is all about. It offers a unique blend of travel and volunteer work, allowing you to immerse yourself in a new culture while contributing to local projects. It's more than just sightseeing—it's about giving back and forming deeper connections with the people and places you visit. You might find yourself teaching English in a remote village, helping build homes, or assisting in wildlife conservation efforts. The benefits are immense: you gain a deeper understanding of the local way of life, make lasting friendships, and come home with a sense of accomplishment and purpose. However, it's not all sunshine and rainbows. The challenges include adjusting to different living conditions, facing cultural differences, and dealing with language barriers. But these hurdles make the experience even more rewarding.

Voluntourism offers countless opportunities across the globe, from rural villages to bustling cities, with each destination providing unique experiences and challenges. In **Costa Rica**, for example, you can contribute to wildlife conservation projects, helping to protect endangered species like sea turtles. If you're passionate about education, **Tanzania** offers chances to teach English in local schools or assist with community development initiatives. In **Nepal**, you might support rebuilding efforts in remote villages affected by natural disasters or working in orphanages to improve the lives of children. For those interested in environmental work, **Australia** offers conservation projects that help restore natural habitats and protect native wildlife.

Several organizations specialize in connecting travelers with voluntourism opportunities. Please refer to the **Resources Chapter** for the list of some of the reputable organizations.

Choosing the right program is crucial. Start by identifying your skills and interests. Are you a retired teacher who loves working with children? Look for programs focused on education. Maybe you're passionate about wildlife—there are plenty of conservation projects that could use your help. Research the organization thoroughly. Check reviews, ask about the nature of the work, and ensure they follow ethical practices. Some organizations might exploit local communities or volunteers, so it's essential to choose one that genuinely benefits both parties. Consider the duration of the stay, too. Some programs last a few weeks, while others can extend to several months. Pick one that fits your schedule and energy levels.

Proper preparation is important for a successful voluntourism experience. Start with the basics: make sure your passport is up to date, and research visa requirements for your destination. Vaccinations might be necessary depending on where you're going. Mental and physical preparation is equally important. You might be working in challenging environments, so it's essential to be in good health and have the right mindset. Training sessions provided by the organization can equip you with the necessary skills and knowledge. They might offer online courses or in-person workshops to prepare you for the work ahead. Packing the right gear, including comfortable clothing and any specific equipment needed for your tasks, ensures you're ready for the adventure.

Once you're on the ground, making the most of your experience involves fully engaging with the local community and culture. Start by learning some basic phrases in the local language—it's a gesture that's always appreciated and can help break the ice. Building genuine relationships with fellow volunteers and locals can enrich your experience immeasurably. Don't be shy—join in local activities, share meals, and listen to their stories. These interactions offer a deeper understanding of the culture and leave you with friendships that last long after you've returned home. Keep a journal to document your experiences, reflections, and the people you meet. This not only helps you process the experience but also creates a wonderful keepsake to look back on. If you enjoy sharing your adventures, your journal entries can serve as the foundation for a blog, vlog, or YouTube channel, allowing you to inspire others with your voluntourism journey. By turning your personal reflections into public content, you can connect with a broader audience and encourage more people to get involved in meaningful travel experiences.

5.3 Senior Safari Adventures: Planning the Trip of a Lifetime

Safaris offer an unforgettable way to experience wildlife and nature up close, with different types catering to various interests and travel styles. Whether you're interested in a traditional drive through sprawling savannahs, a walking safari that lets you explore on foot, or a boat safari along rivers and lakes, each option provides a unique perspective on the natural world. Many safaris also incorporate conservation efforts, giving you the chance to contribute to protecting these precious ecosystems. It's not just about witnessing wildlife—it's about being immersed in the rhythm of nature and supporting the environments that sustain it.

The first step in planning your safari is choosing the right type. Walking safaris offer an immersive experience where you can feel the earth beneath your feet and hear the subtle sounds of nature. However, they require a good level of fitness and stamina. **Zambia's South Luangwa National Park** is renowned for its expertly guided walking safaris, offering a chance to track wildlife while learning about the flora and fauna up close. In **Zimbabwe, Mana Pools National Park** also provides exceptional walking safari experiences along the Zambezi River.

If you prefer a more relaxed approach, vehicle-based tours provide comfort while still offering breathtaking views of wildlife. Destinations like **Kenya's Masai Mara, Tanzania's Serengeti, South Africa's Kruger National Park, and Namibia's Etosha National Park** are popular choices. Each offers unique landscapes and wildlife, ensuring an unforgettable adventure.

If a boating safari piques your interest, consider exploring the winding waterways of **Botswana's Okavango Delta**, where you can observe wildlife from a traditional mokoro (canoe). Another excellent option is a boat safari through **Sri Lanka's Gal Oya National Park**, where you can watch elephants swimming between islands in one of the country's largest reservoirs.

Preparation is key to a successful safari. Start with vaccinations—consult your doctor about necessary shots, such as those for yellow fever and typhoid. Some countries also require malaria prophylaxis. Check visa requirements well in advance; some destinations allow visas on arrival, while others require pre-approval. Pack smartly: lightweight, neutral-colored clothing is best for blending into the environment. Don't forget sturdy and comfortable walking shoes. Depending on the climate, you might need a warm jacket for chilly mornings and evenings. A good camera and binoculars are must-haves for capturing those once-in-a-lifetime moments.

Staying healthy and safe during your safari is paramount. Hydration is crucial, especially in hot climates, so carry a reusable water bottle and drink plenty of fluids. Equally important is protecting yourself from the sun—wear a broad-spectrum sunscreen, a wide-brimmed hat, and sunglasses, and seek shade during the hottest parts of the day. Use insect repellent to protect against bites, and wear long sleeves and pants during dawn and dusk when mosquitoes are most active. Ensure your travel insurance covers medical emergencies in remote areas; it's worth the peace of mind. Familiarize yourself with local health facilities and emergency contacts. Following these precautions will help you enjoy your safari without worrying about health issues.

To maximize your safari experience, consider hiring knowledgeable local guides. Their expertise can transform your trip, offering insights into animal behavior and local ecosystems. Engage in conservation efforts or community visits to deepen your connection with the area. Some tours offer opportunities to visit local schools or partake in wildlife preservation projects. These activities will enrich your experience and contribute positively to the communities you visit, making your safari more impactful and memorable.

5.4 Sea Voyages and River Cruises: Unlocking Unforgettable Adventures

Lounging on the deck of a cruise ship with the horizon stretching before you is the perfect start to a memorable journey. Cruises have become increasingly popular, especially with retirees, for good reason. They offer a convenient and stress-free way to explore multiple destinations without the hassle of packing and unpacking at every stop. With everything from gourmet dining to entertainment, fitness centers, and even medical facilities onboard, cruises cater to every need, allowing travelers to unwind and savor the experience. For retirees, cruises also provide a chance to meet like-minded travelers, join special interest groups, and take part in organized activities, adding a social and enriching dimension to the trip. Whether you prefer a smaller, more intimate ship or the wide range of amenities found on larger vessels, the options are endless, making it easy to find the perfect cruise for your interests and lifestyle.

Selecting the right cruise is crucial to making this dream a reality. Start by considering the size of the ship. Larger ships offer a plethora of activities and dining options but can be overwhelming. Smaller ships provide a more intimate experience and easier navigation.

Look for cruises that cater specifically to seniors, offering a wide range of activities like dance classes, lectures, and wellness programs, including yoga, meditation, and gentle exercise classes tailored to different fitness levels. You'll often find enrichment programs such as cooking demonstrations, wine tastings, and cultural workshops. For those seeking intellectual stimulation, cruises offer guest speakers, educational seminars, and destination-focused talks. There are often opportunities for card games, trivia competitions, and bridge tournaments, creating a sense of community onboard.

Medical facilities are a must—ensure the ship has a well-equipped medical center and staff. Special accommodations like accessible cabins and priority boarding can make your trip even more comfortable.

Ocean cruise destinations like the **Mediterranean, Caribbean,** and **Alaska** are popular for their stunning views and rich cultural experiences.

In the **Mediterranean**, you can explore historic cities like **Rome, Barcelona,** and **Athens**, each offering ancient landmarks and vibrant local culture. **Rome** is famous for its ancient ruins and art museums, while **Barcelona** dazzles with Gaudí's architecture, and **Athens** offers a glimpse into the cradle of Western civilization. **Santorini** enchants with its iconic white-washed buildings and stunning sunsets over the Aegean Sea, while **Mykonos** offers a lively atmosphere with beautiful beaches and vibrant nightlife. **Dubrovnik**, known as the "Pearl of the Adriatic," boasts medieval walls and breathtaking coastal views. **Istanbul**, where East meets West, is rich with Byzantine and Ottoman history, offering landmarks like the Hagia Sophia and Grand Bazaar. **Venice**, with its romantic canals, and **Cannes,** home to the famous film festival, bring their charm to the Mediterranean. Each destination is a gateway to the region's rich history, culture, and unforgettable landscapes.

The **Caribbean** offers tropical paradises such as **St. Lucia, the Bahamas,** and **Aruba**, known for their crystal-clear waters and beautiful beaches. **St. Lucia**, with its dramatic Piton mountains, lush rainforests, and natural hot springs, makes a perfect destination for both relaxation and adventure. **The Bahamas**, with its famous pink sand beaches and vibrant coral reefs, is a haven for snorkeling, diving, and wildlife enthusiasts, offering encounters with dolphins and sea turtles. **Aruba,** often called "One Happy Island," boasts year-round sunshine, stunning white-sand beaches, and colorful colonial architecture, blending Caribbean charm with Dutch influences. Each island offers a unique mix of natural beauty, culture, and activities, from exploring local markets to lounging in secluded coves.

For breathtaking natural beauty, cruises to **Alaska** often include stops in **Glacier Bay** and **Juneau**, where you can witness glaciers and wildlife up close. Other popular cruise destinations include **Norway's Shores & Fjords**, where dramatic cliffs and waterfalls line the coastline, and **New Zealand's Milford Sound**, offering awe-inspiring landscapes. The **Baltic Sea** is a cultural treasure trove, with stops in cities like **Helsinki** and **Oslo**, where you can delve into Viking history and explore Scandinavian heritage. Don't miss the chance to witness the Northern Lights on a cruise to **Norway** or **Iceland**, offering one of nature's most spectacular displays. **Tallinn, Stockholm**, and **Copenhagen** provide fascinating glimpses into the art, architecture, and history of **Northern Europe**.

River cruises offer a unique way to experience the culture and history of a destination. As you sail down iconic rivers like the **Danube, Rhine, or Seine**, the landscape unfolds before you—castles perched on hilltops, vineyards lining the banks, and charming villages with cobbled streets and vibrant markets. River cruising tends to be more immersive, with ports of call often located in the heart of cities, allowing for easy and quick access to local landmarks and attractions.

These cruises are also known for their inclusive excursions, with many offering guided tours of historical sites, UNESCO World Heritage landmarks, and local cultural experiences. You can visit historic castles along the **Rhine**, explore the art-filled museums of **Amsterdam**, or sip wine in the vineyards of **France's Bordeaux region**—all while enjoying the comforts of your floating hotel.

River cruises also offer the chance to attend onboard lectures and cultural performances, enhancing your understanding of the region you're visiting. On a **Mekong River** cruise, for instance, you might watch traditional Apsara dances or listen to local musicians. Cruises along the **Nile** provide access to ancient Egyptian temples and pyramids, with expert guides explaining the mysteries of the pharaohs.

Staying healthy and safe on a cruise starts with food safety. Stick to bottled water and be cautious with buffet-style dining. Motion sickness can put a damper on the party, but you can manage it with remedies like ginger tablets or acupressure wristbands. Navigating the ship safely is essential; wear non-slip shoes and use handrails when moving around. Many cruise lines offer mobility aids like wheelchairs and scooters for rent. These small precautions can ensure you enjoy your trip with no hiccups. Shore excursions can be thrilling but choose wisely. Opt for guided tours that offer a balance of adventure and relaxation. Safety is key, so stick with group tours and always have a map and local emergency numbers handy.

Budgeting for a cruise can be a balancing act. All-inclusive packages might seem pricey upfront but can save you money in the long run by covering meals, activities, and excursions. Look for senior discounts and special promotions. Booking during off-peak times can also score you significant savings. When choosing a cruise company, it's essential to do some research. Start by reading customer reviews on trusted travel websites like **CruiseCritic** or **TripAdvisor** to get a sense of other travelers' experiences. Pay attention to feedback on the quality of service, cleanliness, and onboard activities. Opt for companies with a strong reputation for safety and customer satisfaction like **Expedia, TripAdvisor, CruiseDirect, CruiseWatch**. Avoid cruise lines with frequent complaints about hidden fees, poor service, or overcrowding. Make sure the company is transparent about what's included in the price—watch out for extra charges for gratuities, Wi-Fi, or premium dining. If possible, talk to friends or family who have cruised with the company to get firsthand recommendations. Last, check for the cruise line's sustainability efforts; companies that prioritize eco-friendly practices often provide a more conscientious travel experience.

5.5 Top Historical Landmarks for Your Global Bucket List

Exploring the ruins of ancient civilizations is like taking a journey through time, where each destination offers a unique glimpse into humanity's rich and diverse history. The thrill of standing where empires once flourished, where ancient leaders ruled, and where age-old stories were born is something that can only be truly appreciated in person. History comes alive when you walk through these iconic sites, immersing yourself in the grandeur of past civilizations.

The **Pyramids of Giza**, rising majestically from the sands of Egypt, are a testament to the ingenuity and ambition of the pharaohs. In **Rome, the Colosseum**, still towering over the city, echoes with the legacy of gladiatorial combat and the roaring crowds of ancient times. High in the **Andes, Machu Picchu** invites you into the sophisticated world of the Inca Empire, with its intricately designed terraces and temples. The **Acropolis of Athens** remains a symbol of Greek democracy and culture, while the **Great Wall of China** stretches endlessly across the landscape, a marvel of ancient engineering and defense. In **England**, the mysterious **Stonehenge** continues to intrigue visitors with its ancient origins and purpose.

Other must-visit historical destinations include **Petra in Jordan**, an ancient city carved into rose-red cliffs that served as a vital crossroads of trade, and **Angkor Wat in Cambodia**, the largest religious monument in the world, showcasing the grandeur of the Khmer Empire. The ancient city of **Pompeii in Italy**, preserved under volcanic ash, provides an incredibly detailed snapshot of life in the Roman Empire. The temples of **Luxor in Egypt** reveal millennia of Egyptian history, while **Kyoto in Japan** offers a window into the country's imperial past with its centuries-old temples and palaces. Each of these places carries stories, legends, and an aura that can only be truly appreciated in person.

Planning visits to these historical sites involves a bit of strategizing to make the most of your experience. Early mornings or late afternoons are often the best times to visit to avoid the swarms of tourists and the midday heat. Many sites offer senior discounts on tickets, so don't forget to inquire or check online beforehand. Guided tours can enrich your visit with fascinating anecdotes and deeper insights, making the history come alive. Whether it's a small group tour or a private guide, having an expert by your side can transform your visit from a simple sightseeing trip into an educational adventure.

Navigating historical sites requires a bit of preparation, especially considering the physical demands they might pose. Uneven surfaces, steep climbs, and extensive walking are common. Look for sites that provide amenities like benches for resting, accessible pathways, and shuttle services. Comfortable, supportive footwear is a must. Carry a small, lightweight backpack with essentials like water, a hat, sunscreen, and any necessary medications. Taking breaks and pacing yourself ensures you can enjoy the experience without overexerting.

I remember our trip to Pompeii vividly. We hadn't anticipated just how enormous the site was, nor did we fully appreciate the challenges posed by its ancient sidewalks. I was wearing sandals that weren't particularly comfortable, and we hadn't packed any snacks or extra water. By the time we reached the end of our tour, we were completely exhausted. Though the experience of walking through this incredibly well-preserved Roman city was stunning, we weren't able to see as much as we had hoped because of our lack of preparation. The vast scale of Pompeii, combined with the uneven stone streets, made it far more physically demanding than expected. Next time, we'll definitely be better prepared with sturdy shoes and snacks so I can fully take in the wonder of such a remarkable place.

Preserving memories of these visits can be as enriching as the visits themselves. Photography is a fantastic way to capture the beauty and details of each site. Journaling adds another layer, allowing you to reflect on your experiences and emotions. Blogging or vlogging lets you document your travels in real-time, creating a dynamic way to capture memories and inspire others with your stories. Before you go, immerse yourself in documentaries, books, or online courses about the sites you'll visit. This pre-visit education can deepen your appreciation, making the trip even more fulfilling.

5.6 Cultural European Tours for the Curious Retiree

Imagine strolling through the cobbled streets of **Prague**, each corner revealing a new piece of history, or standing in awe before the masterpieces of the **Louvre in Paris**. Planning a cultural tour in Europe starts with choosing destinations rich in history and art. **Florence, Italy**, with its Renaissance treasures, and **Vienna, Austria**, known for its classical music heritage, are must-visits.

Don't overlook hidden gems like **Bruges in Belgium**, a medieval town that feels like stepping into a fairy tale, or **Porto in Portugal**, where vibrant culture and stunning architecture await. For a unique experience, head to **Munich, Germany**, during Oktoberfest, where you can enjoy lively beer halls, traditional Bavarian music, and hearty local cuisine. Other amazing destinations include the charming town of **Rothenburg ob der Tauber in Germany**, with its perfectly preserved medieval architecture, and **Dresden**, a city rich in baroque splendor.

For classical music lovers, **Salzburg, Austria**, the birthplace of Mozart, offers an enchanting atmosphere with its beautiful baroque architecture and the annual **Salzburg Festival** celebrating his legacy. In cities like **Graz, Austria,** and **Girona, Spain**, you'll find fewer tourists and a more intimate feel, with stunning architecture and rich histories that rival more famous destinations.

Imagine wandering through the ancient streets of **Bath, England**, where Roman baths and Georgian architecture transport you back in time. England is rich in cultural sites like **Canterbury Cathedral**, a UNESCO World Heritage Site that showcases stunning Gothic architecture, and **Oxford**, home to the world-renowned university and charming historic buildings. In **Scotland**, a visit to **Edinburgh Castle** offers panoramic views of the city and a deep dive into Scotland's turbulent history. For something truly mystical, explore the **Isle of Skye**, where rugged landscapes and ancient clan traditions are still alive, while **Glasgow** boasts a vibrant arts scene and impressive Victorian architecture.

France is home to more than just the Louvre. In **Normandy**, visit the stunning **Mont Saint-Michel**, a medieval abbey perched on a tidal island. In the south, explore the **Palace of the Popes** in Avignon, a UNESCO site with fascinating papal history. **Strasbourg**, with its blend of French and German influences, offers a unique cultural experience. And don't forget the **Château de Chambord** in the Loire Valley, a true marvel of Renaissance architecture. While you're in the area, make sure to visit **Château de Chenonceau,** famously spanning the River Cher with its stunning arches, and **Château de Villandry**, known for its magnificent Renaissance gardens. Further along the Loire, you'll find **Château d'Amboise,** where Leonardo da Vinci spent his final years. Each of these castles offers a unique glimpse into France's regal past, with enchanting architecture, lush landscapes, and fascinating history waiting to be explored.

In Italy, beyond Florence's Renaissance treasures, explore the Amalfi Coast for breathtaking views of dramatic cliffs, sparkling seas, and charming seaside villages like Positano and Ravello. Ravello, in particular, is known not only for its stunning gardens and panoramic views but also for its annual Ravello Festival, a prestigious musical event held each summer that brings classical music performances to its open-air venues. For a quieter escape, head to Verona, the city of Romeo and Juliet, where you can visit Juliet's famous balcony and wander through Roman ruins, including a well-preserved amphitheater still used for operas today.

Siena offers a step back in time with its preserved medieval streets, impressive cathedral, and the thrilling Palio horse race held twice a year in the historic Piazza del Campo. Further south, Naples provides a gateway to ancient history with the nearby ruins of Pompeii and Herculaneum, frozen in time by the eruption of Mount Vesuvius. Don't miss Sicily, where Greek temples like those in Agrigento's Valley of the Temples blend seamlessly with Roman villas, Baroque architecture, and lively markets. In Sicily's capital, Palermo, you can explore a rich tapestry of cultural influences, from Norman palaces to bustling street food stalls. Whether you're drawn to Italy's art, architecture, or history, every region offers its own distinct and captivating experience.

For a different vibe, visit **Split, Croatia**, where the ancient **Diocletian's Palace** meets vibrant modern life, or **Zagreb**, a city full of Austro-Hungarian charm with bustling markets and beautiful parks. In **Hungary**, **Budapest** is a must-visit with its thermal baths, stunning **Parliament Building**, and the **Buda Castle** overlooking the Danube River. **Turkey** offers a captivating blend of ancient and modern worlds. In **Istanbul**, you'll be mesmerized by landmarks like the **Hagia Sophia**, **Topkapi Palace**, and the bustling **Grand Bazaar**. Don't miss the chance to visit **Ephesus**, one of the best-preserved ancient cities, showcasing the grandeur of Roman architecture. **Bulgaria**, with its hidden gems, is an underrated cultural destination. The ancient capital, **Veliko Tarno-**

vo, offers a glimpse into medieval Bulgarian history, while the **Rila Monastery**, a UNESCO World Heritage Site, is a masterpiece of Bulgarian art and architecture.

In the Baltics, **Estonia** is a country where medieval charm meets cutting-edge technology. **Tallinn**, the capital, boasts one of the best-preserved medieval towns in Europe, with its cobblestone streets, historic towers, and Gothic spires. In the Netherlands, explore **Amsterdam**, where you can marvel at the masterpieces of **Van Gogh** and **Rembrandt** in the **Rijksmuseum**, or take a peaceful canal cruise through the city's scenic waterways. The **Keukenhof Gardens**, with their **world-famous tulip displays**, are a must-see in spring, offering a colorful and quintessentially Dutch experience.

For those who prefer a leisurely pace, senior-friendly tour options are abundant. Companies like **Road Scholar** and **Saga Holidays** offer packages tailored to seniors, focusing on slower-paced itineraries with ample rest periods. These tours often include skip-the-line tickets to major attractions, ensuring you spend more time enjoying and less time queuing. Group sizes are usually smaller, providing a more intimate and personalized experience. Whether it's a four-week grand tour of Europe or a quick getaway to a single city, these packages take the stress out of planning and allow you to immerse yourself fully in the cultural experience.

Engaging with local culture can turn a pleasant trip into an unforgettable one. Learn a few basic phrases in the local language—simple greetings and polite phrases go a long way. Familiarize yourself with local customs; for instance, in Spain, it's common to greet people with a kiss on each cheek, and in Germany, don't forget to clink your beer glasses and say "Prost!" at Oktoberfest. Try the local cuisine, whether it's sampling tapas in Barcelona, pierogi in Poland, gelato in Rome, or indulging in bratwurst and pretzels in Germany. Take part in local festivals or cultural events and don't be shy about interacting with locals. They can offer insights and recommendations that you won't find in any guidebook.

Maximizing the experience of your cultural tour involves a bit of strategic planning. Visit major sites early in the morning or late in the afternoon to avoid crowds. Guided tours can provide deeper insights and often include access to areas not open to the general public. Seek out hidden spots known only to locals—those charming cafes tucked away in alleys, or small museums that house incredible collections. Take your time to savor each moment, whether it's enjoying a leisurely lunch at a sidewalk café or sitting quietly in a centuries-old cathedral. Your golden years are the perfect time to explore the rich tapestry of Europe's cultural heritage.

Themed cultural tours

A few years ago, my husband and I decided to take a cultural tour focused on the life of Mozart, our favorite composer. We envisioned this trip as a way to immerse ourselves in the rich musical history of Europe while exploring some of its most beautiful cities. Our journey began in **Prague**, a city that, while not a primary residence of Mozart, held a special place in his heart. We attended a performance of *The Marriage of Figaro* at the **Estates Theatre**, where Mozart conducted the world premiere of his famous opera Don Giovanni in 1787. Sitting in the historic auditorium, we experienced the same venue where Mozart once captivated audiences with his genius. The performance was breathtaking, and knowing that scenes from the movie *Amadeus* were filmed in this theater added an extra layer of historical significance. Watching the opera in such a meaningful and beautiful setting made it one of the most memorable experiences of our trip. Another highlight of our visit to Prague was exploring **Bertramka**, a historic villa where Mozart stayed during his visits to the city. This charming estate, now a museum, was once the residence of the Dušek family, close friends of Mozart. Here, he reportedly completed *Don Giovanni* just days before its premiere.

From Prague, we rented a car and drove to **Vienna**, the true heart of our Mozart pilgrimage. Once in Vienna, we dove headfirst into the rich history of classical music. We visited the **Mozarthaus**, Mozart's former residence, which is now a museum dedicated to his life and works. The feeling of walking through the same rooms where Mozart composed some of his greatest masterpieces was simply awe-inspiring. We also attended a concert at the **Vienna State Opera**, and it was a mesmerizing experience. The city's blend of imperial grandeur, music, and art made every moment feel like stepping into a living museum.

From Vienna, we decided to take the scenic route rather than the bustling Autobahn, driving along the **Danube River** as we made our way to **Salzburg**, Mozart's birthplace. This slower pace allowed us to stop in charming towns like **Melk** and **Dürnstein**, each offering its own unique slice of Austrian history and culture. We spent time at the **Melk Abbey**, a baroque masterpiece perched above the Danube, and wandered through the picturesque vineyards surrounding the river, soaking in the tranquility of the countryside.

In **Salzburg**, we visited the **Mozart Residence** and his birthplace on **Getreidegasse**, both now museums, offering a deeper understanding of his early life. We also explored the **Salzburg Cathedral**, where Mozart was baptized, and **St. Peter's Abbey**, where he composed some of his early works. The **Hohensalzburg Fortress**, towering over the city, provided us with breathtaking views of the surrounding Alps and a chance to immerse ourselves in centuries of history. The fortress, with its medieval architecture and panoramic views, was awe-inspiring on its own, but our experience there was made even more special by attending an intimate chamber orchestra concert within its historic halls. The music, echoing through the fortress, created an unforgettable atmosphere, transporting us back to the times when Salzburg was alive with the sound of classical compositions. To top off the evening, we indulged in a romantic dinner at the fortress, dining on Austrian cuisine as the city below sparkled with lights. The combination of history, music, and a beautifully prepared meal created one of the most enchanting nights of our trip, blending the past and present in a truly magical way.

Of course, we couldn't miss exploring the sites where **The Sound of Music** was filmed. Wandering through the **Mirabell Gardens**, where the famous "Do-Re-Mi" scene was shot, brought back memories of the beloved musical. Walking along the same paths, surrounded by vibrant flowers and framed by the fortress in the background, gave us a sense of nostalgia and connection to Salzburg's cinematic legacy. The film's iconic settings, scattered throughout the city, added another layer of charm and history to our visit, making our journey through Salzburg a delightful blend of music, film, and history.

Though not directly tied to Mozart, we couldn't resist making a stop in the medieval town of **Český Krumlov** on our way back to **Prague**. Nestled in the Czech countryside, this UNESCO World Heritage Site, with its winding streets and fairy-tale castle, was like stepping into another time. Wandering through its streets, we were reminded of how much history and culture Europe has to offer at every turn.

This journey not only deepened our appreciation for Mozart and classical music but also enriched our understanding of European history and culture. The opportunity to explore these cities at our own pace, venturing off the beaten path and connecting with local traditions, was an unforgettable experience. If you're considering a cultural tour of Europe, I highly recommend planning around the figures and places that resonate with you—whether it's music, art, history, or food—and taking the time to savor each stop along the way.

While my husband and I planned our Mozart-inspired cultural tour at our own pace, there are countless other themed cultural tours in Europe that cater to a wide range of interests. If you prefer to have your itinerary set, or just want the convenience of a guided experience, many companies specialize in themed cultural tours that allow you to explore Europe's rich history, art, and traditions. Here are a few themed cultural tours you might want to consider:

Shakespeare's England: Literary Tour of the UK

If you are a lover of literature, a tour of Shakespeare's England is a must. Starting in **Stratford-upon-Avon**, the birthplace of William Shakespeare, you can visit his childhood home, the school where he studied, and the **Royal Shakespeare Theatre**, where his works are still performed. The tour can take you to **London**, where you can experience the **Globe Theatre**, a replica of Shakespeare's original theater. Nearby, **Oxford** offers its own literary charm, home to great authors like J.R.R. Tolkien and Lewis Carroll. For those wanting an immersive literary journey, many companies offer guided tours that include stops at Shakespeare's haunts, as well as performances of his plays.

Impressionist Art in France

Art lovers can take a trip through the heart of **France**, visiting key locations that inspired the great Impressionist painters. Start in **Paris**, where you can explore the **Musée d'Orsay**, home to masterpieces by **Monet, Degas, and Renoir**. Travel to **Giverny**, where you can visit **Monet's house and gardens**, immortalized in his famous water lily series. A stop in **Rouen**, known for its beautiful cathedral often painted by **Monet**, can round out this art-lovers pilgrimage.

The Viking Trail: Scandinavia's Rich Heritage

For those fascinated by ancient history and mythology, a tour tracing the Viking legacy through **Norway**, **Denmark**, and **Sweden** offers a deep dive into the Norse culture. Visit **Oslo's Viking Ship Museum,** tour **Roskilde** in Denmark where Viking ships were built, and explore the ancient trading town of **Birka** in Sweden. Companies like **Viking River Cruises** often combine these historical experiences with scenic voyages along the fjords and rivers that Vikings once traversed, making it both an educational and visually stunning journey.

Music Lovers' Vienna to Leipzig Tour

If classical music is your passion, a tour from **Vienna, Austria**, to **Leipzig, Germany,** offers an opportunity to explore the lives and works of some of the greatest composers. **Vienna**, with its rich musical heritage, is home to museums dedicated to **Beethoven and Schubert**, as well as the legendary **Vienna State Opera**. It's also the city where **Johann Strauss**, the "Waltz King," composed many of his most famous works. You can visit the **Strauss Residence,** now a museum, where he lived and composed the iconic *Blue Danube* waltz. From there, travel to **Leipzig,** where **Bach** spent much of his life. You can visit **St. Thomas Church,** where Bach was choirmaster, and the **Bach Museum.** Along the way, you might also explore **Salzburg,** Mozart's birthplace, and **Bayreuth,** where Wagner's famous opera festival takes place. This journey through Europe's musical history offers a harmonious blend of cultural discovery and melodic inspiration.

Ancient Civilizations Tour: Greece and Italy

History buffs can embark on a journey through the cradle of Western civilization by visiting the ruins of ancient **Greece** and **Italy**. Begin in **Athens,** exploring the **Acropolis,** the **Parthenon,** and ancient theaters, before heading to the island of **Delphi,** home of the Oracle. Then make your way to **Rome,** where you'll walk through history at the **Colosseum,** the **Roman Forum,** and the awe-inspiring **Pantheon.** Don't miss the lesser-known, but equally remarkable, site of **Paestum** in **Southern Italy.** This ancient city, originally founded by the Greeks, boasts some of the best-preserved Greek temples in the world. The three colossal temples dedicated to Hera and Athena rival the grandeur of those in Athens, and the site offers a quieter, more reflective atmosphere. For a more immersive experience, companies such as **Road Scholar** or **Odyssey Traveller** offer small group tours, complete with expert historians to guide you through ancient relics and architecture.

5.7 Learning While Traveling: Cultural Exchange Programs

Cultural exchange programs offer a unique and enriching way to travel, allowing you to deeply immerse yourself in a new culture while gaining firsthand experience in local traditions. Unlike typical sightseeing trips, cultural exchanges provide opportunities for language immersion, culinary lessons, art workshops, and homestays, giving you a deeper, more personal understanding of the culture you're visiting. Whether you're learning to cook authentic local dishes, participating in traditional festivals, or engaging in daily life with a host family, these experiences provide a rich, personal connection to the people and customs of a foreign country. For retirees, cultural exchange programs are an excellent way to combine travel with learning, offering not only new skills and knowledge but also meaningful connections that often lead to lifelong friendships.

Selecting the right cultural exchange program requires careful research, especially when looking for options tailored to older adults. Start by considering your interests and goals—do you want to focus on learning languages, history, arts, or something else entirely? Once you've narrowed down your interests, look for reputable programs through established organizations. Programs like **Road Scholar, GoAbroad**, and **Global Volunteers** offer a variety of cultural exchange opportunities specifically designed for older adults. It's important to consider factors like the duration of the program (whether it's a short-term stay or an extended cultural immersion), the level of support services provided (such as language assistance or emergency contacts), and the reviews of past participants. Many exchange programs provide accommodations like homestays or local apartments, so you'll also want to look into the housing options and see if they fit your comfort level. Reading participant testimonials can give you a clearer idea of the experience and ensure the program is trustworthy and well-run.

Proper preparation is essential to make the most of your cultural exchange experience. Start by learning some basic phrases in the local language to help with daily communication—simple greetings, polite phrases, and common questions go a long way in showing respect for the culture you're entering. You can use apps like **Duolingo** or **Babbel** to get a head start. Conducting some cultural research ahead of time is also helpful. Familiarize yourself with the country's customs, etiquette, and traditions to avoid cultural faux pas and better appreciate your experiences. Planning the logistics for an extended stay is another important step. This includes securing the proper visas, ensuring your passport is up to date, and obtaining travel insurance. Make sure to pack thoughtfully, considering the climate, local dress codes, and any specialized items you might need for your cultural activities. Preparing mentally for an extended stay abroad—being open to new experiences and flexible with any challenges—will also help ensure a rewarding experience.

Please refer to the **Resources Chapter** for a list of reputable organizations offering cultural exchange programs.

5.8 Savoring the World Through Food and Wine Adventures

Food and wine travel offers a rich, sensory way to experience the world, allowing you to immerse yourself in local culture through its cuisine and regional wines. This type of travel provides a perfect blend of indulgence and education, whether you're strolling through vineyards, taking part in cooking classes, or dining at local restaurants. The joy of tasting authentic dishes paired with locally produced wines gives you a deep appreciation for the history and traditions behind them. For retirees, food and wine travel is an ideal way to engage your senses, expand your culinary knowledge, and enjoy new destinations in a relaxing yet enriching way.

There are countless destinations around the world where food and wine lovers can indulge in culinary delights. **Italy** is a classic choice for both food and wine enthusiasts, offering experiences such as tasting Chianti in **Tuscany**, enjoying pasta in **Bologna**, or learning to make traditional pizza in **Naples**. In the picturesque countryside, you can explore vineyards, enjoy truffle hunts, and participate in pasta-making classes with local chefs. **France** is another premier destination, famous for its rich culinary traditions and world-renowned wines. In regions like **Bordeaux and Burgundy**, you can tour vineyards, sip fine wine, and enjoy gourmet meals that showcase local flavors. **Paris** is a haven for food lovers, offering Michelin-starred dining, bustling markets, and intimate patisseries.

For those seeking more exotic flavors, **Spain** offers a blend of vibrant cuisine and outstanding wines. Tapas tours through cities like **Seville or Barcelona** are a fantastic way to sample regional specialties, while a trip to the **La Rioja** wine region lets you savor some of Spain's best wines.

Argentina is another excellent destination for food and wine travel, particularly for those who love steak and Malbec. In **Mendoza**, you can tour vineyards set against the backdrop of the Andes and enjoy world-class wines paired with traditional Argentine dishes.

In the USA, **Napa Valley in California** is an iconic wine region known for its exquisite wines and farm-to-table dining experiences. Pairing locally sourced meals with Napa's famous Cabernet Sauvignon is a quintessential American food and wine experience. **Sonoma** offers a slightly more relaxed vibe but with equally high-quality wines. For a different kind of food and wine experience, **New Orleans** blends Creole and Cajun flavors with a lively atmosphere and some of the best food festivals in the country. In **Oregon**, you'll find excellent Pinot Noir wines in the **Willamette Valley**, paired with fresh seafood and locally grown produce.

South Africa's food and wine scene is a hidden gem waiting to be explored. The **Western Cape**, particularly **Stellenbosch** and **Franschhoek**, offers world-class vineyards set against breathtaking mountain backdrops. Here, you can indulge in award-winning wines like Pinotage and Chenin Blanc, paired with farm-to-table cuisine that highlights the region's fresh, local produce. Wine estates often offer guided tours, tastings, and gourmet meals, allowing visitors to immerse themselves in the rich culinary heritage of South Africa. **Cape Town** is another must-visit, with its vibrant food markets, top-tier restaurants, and coastal views that make every dining experience unforgettable.

Australia's food and wine regions are as vast and diverse as its landscapes. The **Barossa Valley**, just outside **Adelaide**, is renowned for its bold Shiraz and other robust red wines. In addition to its acclaimed wineries, the region offers culinary tours where you can sample artisanal cheeses, olive oils, and fresh produce straight from the farm. For those seeking a coastal wine experience, the **Margaret River** in **Western Australia** provides both world-class vineyards and stunning beaches. **Melbourne** and **Sydney** are home to vibrant food scenes with markets, award-winning restaurants, and cultural diversity that bring a wide array of global flavors to the table.

In Canada, the **Naramata Bench** wine region in British Columbia's Okanagan Valley is a hidden gem that rivals some of the world's best wine destinations. Nestled along the eastern shores of **Okanagan Lake**, this area boasts not only award-winning wines but also stunning landscapes, perfect for a relaxing and scenic getaway. Known for its small boutique wineries, Naramata offers a laid-back atmosphere where you can chat with winemakers, sip exceptional Pinot Gris or Syrah, and take in breathtaking lake views all at once. The region is also a paradise for food lovers, with farm-to-table restaurants serving fresh, local produce that pairs beautifully with the region's wines. Living in British Columbia, my husband and I have spent several vacations exploring the Naramata region, and even after multiple visits, we feel like we've only scratched the surface of what this magical place has to offer. We'd spend our days cycling between vineyards, and our evenings unwinding by the lake, watching the sunset over the Okanagan. Beyond the wine, the area offers great opportunities for hiking, swimming, and enjoying the pristine beauty of the Okanagan Valley.

When planning a food and wine travel experience, it's important to find the right combination that matches your preferences. Some travelers prefer guided culinary and wine tours, where local experts take you through the best vineyards, restaurants, and markets, explaining the history and nuances behind every dish and glass of wine. Others might enjoy a more hands-on experience, such as cooking classes paired with wine tastings, where you learn to prepare local dishes and understand how different wines enhance the flavors. Wine and food festivals are another excellent way to immerse yourself in the local wine culture—events like the **Sonoma Wine Country Weekend** or **Italy's Alba White Truffle Festival** provide the perfect combination of food, wine, and festivity.

If you're seeking something more intimate, vineyard stays offer the chance to live in the heart of a wine region, surrounded by grapevines, where you can meet winemakers and experience the winemaking process firsthand. Many luxury travel companies and specialized food and wine tour operators, such as **Zicasso, Butterfield & Robinson,** and **Culinary Backstreets**, offer customized itineraries that combine the best experiences.

Researching the local cuisine and regional wines before your trip will help you appreciate what you're about to experience. Learning a few basic phrases in the local language can enhance your interactions with chefs, winemakers, and restaurant staff. It's also helpful to pack with food and wine tours in mind—comfortable shoes are essential for walking through vineyards, markets, or cobblestone streets. Consider bringing a wine carrier if you plan to purchase bottles to bring home, or look into shipping services offered by many wineries. Also, don't forget to research customs regulations if you plan on bringing wine or food items home. Ensure you make reservations at highly rated restaurants and popular wineries in advance, especially if you're traveling to renowned food and wine regions during peak seasons. Planning your itinerary to include visits to farmers' markets and local food festivals can offer a chance to taste seasonal ingredients and get a feel for the local food culture.

While indulging in the finest wines during your travels, it's essential to remember that moderation is key, especially for seniors. Many studies suggest that moderate alcohol consumption, particularly red wine, can offer health benefits such as improved cardiovascular health, reduced risk of certain types of heart disease, and increased levels of HDL, the "good" cholesterol. The Mediterranean diet, which includes moderate wine consumption, is often cited for its health benefits, including longevity and reduced inflammation.

For seniors, however, it's important to balance these potential benefits with the risks of overconsumption. While traditional guidelines suggest that moderation means one glass of wine per day for women and up to two for men, recent studies are challenging the idea that even this amount is entirely risk-free. Research now shows that alcohol, even in moderate amounts, may increase the risk of certain diseases, including breast, liver, colon, and esophageal cancer. Alcohol can interfere with the body's ability to absorb essential nutrients, weaken the immune system, and exacerbate chronic conditions like high blood pressure and diabetes. For older adults, it's especially important to consider these risks, as alcohol can interact negatively with medications, impair balance, and contribute to dehydration, increasing the risk of falls and other health complications. When enjoying food and wine travel, it's essential to stay informed about these emerging findings and consider personal health risks when deciding how much alcohol to consume. Savor each sip, but be mindful of your limits to ensure you're maximizing the health benefits without risking adverse effects.

As we conclude our exploration of unforgettable travel destinations and once-in-a-lifetime experiences, it's time to turn up the excitement volume and dive into a world of thrilling adventure. While wandering through ancient cities and relaxing on scenic river cruises can satisfy your soul, some of us, retirees, crave the rush of adrenaline and the challenge of more extreme activities. In the next chapter, we'll explore heart-pounding adventures like hot air ballooning over stunning landscapes, scuba diving into the depths of the ocean, skydiving from dizzying heights, and much more. So, if you're ready to take your retirement to new heights—literally—let's jump into the exhilarating world of adventure and excitement!

6

Sky High & Deep Dive: Adventure-Fueled Experiences

As the ground drops away beneath you, the world stretches out in a stunning panorama, and your heart races—not from fear, but from the thrill of adventure. Welcome to the world of extreme sports, where retirement is just the beginning of new, exhilarating experiences. Whether it's skydiving, paragliding, zip-lining through dense forests, or taking on white-water rapids, these adrenaline-pumping activities can inject excitement into your golden years. Embracing these challenges isn't just about pushing your physical limits—it's about embracing life to the fullest, proving that age is no barrier to adventure.

6.1 Skydiving and Paragliding: Thrills in the Sky

Let's start by understanding the basics. Skydiving and paragliding both offer the thrill of flight, but they're as different as night and day. Skydiving is like jumping straight into an adrenaline rush. You strap on a parachute, board a plane, and at a dizzying height, you leap into the sky. The first few seconds are a free fall, with the wind roaring in your ears, then you pull the cord, and the parachute opens, slowing your descent for a peaceful float down to earth. Paragliding, on the other hand, is gliding gracefully through the air. You take off from a hill or cliff, with a wing-like parachute catching the wind, allowing you to soar gently for miles, enjoying a bird's-eye view of the landscape below. Both require specific equipment: skydiving needs a parachute rig and an altimeter, while paragliding involves a paraglider, harness, and helmet. Beginners in both sports can expect thorough training sessions, usually starting with tandem flights where an instructor handles the technicalities, letting you savor the experience.

Safety first, always! When it comes to skydiving and paragliding, choosing certified and reputable operators is crucial. Look for companies with excellent safety records, glowing reviews, and certifications from recognized bodies like the **United States Parachute Association (USPA)** for skydiving or the **United States Hang Gliding and Paragliding Association (USHPA)** for paragliding. If you're traveling internationally, be sure to research the equivalent certifications in other countries. These certifications will give you peace of mind knowing you're in safe hands, no matter where you are. The operators provide thorough safety briefings, quality equipment, and certified instructors who can guide you through every step of the process. Imagine being paired with an instructor who's logged thousands of jumps or flights—talk about peace of mind! They'll ensure you understand the procedures, from how to handle the equipment to what to do in case of an emergency. Rest assured, reputable companies maintain and inspect their gear rigorously, so you're flying with the best.

Please refer to the **Resources Chapter** for a list of reputable organizations for skydiving and paragliding, along with their websites.

Before you take to the skies, it's essential to consider the physical and health requirements for these activities. Skydiving and paragliding aren't as physically demanding as running a marathon, but they do require a certain level of fitness. Weight limits are in place to ensure safety—typically around 220-240 pounds, though this can vary by operator. If you have heart conditions, severe back issues, or mobility constraints, it's wise to consult your doctor beforehand. Both sports involve short bursts of physical effort and can be exhilarating, which might not be suitable for everyone. But if you're in good health and your doctor gives you the green light, the sky's the limit!

If you're ready to take the plunge or glide through the skies, there's no shortage of breathtaking destinations to choose from. Picture yourself in **Interlaken, Switzerland**, where the snow-capped peaks of the Swiss Alps and stunning views of crystal-clear lakes serve as the backdrop for both skydiving and paragliding. For those seeking adventure at the far edge of the world, **Queenstown, New Zealand,** offers an equally exhilarating experience combining adrenaline-pumping activities with awe-inspiring scenery. If tropical landscapes are more your style, in places like **Maui** and **Oahu**, the lush valleys, volcanic craters, and endless coastline provide a spectacular setting as you leap or glide with the vast Pacific Ocean beneath you. In **Chamonix, France**, you can soar over Europe's highest peaks with Mont Blanc towering in the distance. For an unforgettable mix of city and nature, **Cape Town, South Africa,** offers the best of both worlds. Skydiving here gives you unparalleled views of **Table Mountain**, **Robben Island**, and the ocean. Or, if you prefer a more leisurely adventure, paragliding from **Lion's Head** or **Signal Hill** allows you to take in the iconic scenery with a gentle descent over the stunning landscape. Even urban environments offer their own unique thrill, and **Dubai** is a prime example offering a one-of-a-kind view of the archipelago of artificial islands of **Palm Jumeirah** and the glittering skyline of the city. For those seeking serenity alongside their adventure, the peaceful **Phewa Lake Pokhara in Nepal** is an idyllic destination for paragliding, creating a surreal experience that blends tranquility with exhilaration.

No matter which destination you choose, these iconic locations guarantee that your skydiving or paragliding adventure will be nothing short of spectacular, leaving you with unforgettable memories and stories to tell.

Capturing the moment is a big part of the thrill. Most adventure companies offer video or photo packages that document your experience from start to finish. Imagine showing your grandkids a video of you free-falling through the sky or gliding serenely over a mountain range—they'll think you're the coolest grandparent ever! These packages often include a video of the entire experience, from the nervous anticipation before the jump to the triumphant landing. Some even offer GoPros attached to your helmet, giving you a first-person perspective on your adventure. It's not just about the bragging rights (though that's a perk); it's about reliving the thrill and sharing it with family and friends. So, get ready to strike a pose and let the wind ruffle your hair—a picture-perfect moment awaits.

6.2 Scuba Diving: Exploring Underwater Worlds

Floating weightlessly in a vibrant underwater wonderland, surrounded by colorful fish and intricate coral formations, feels like stepping into another realm. If this sounds like a dream come true, then scuba diving is your ticket to this magical world. To get started, you'll need to obtain a scuba diving certification. Two popular beginner-friendly courses are the **PADI Open Water Diver** and the **NAUI Scuba Diver**. These courses typically involve a mix of classroom study, pool sessions, and open-water dives. You'll learn the fundamental skills, safety procedures, and equipment handling needed for a safe and enjoyable dive. The courses are structured to build your confidence gradually, ensuring that by the time you take your first open water dive, you'll feel like a fish in water.

Selecting the right dive spots is crucial, especially for beginners and older divers. You want locations with calm waters and abundant marine life. Some top destinations include the **Great Barrier Reef in Australia**, known for its breathtaking biodiversity, and **Cozumel in Mexico**, famous for its crystal-clear waters and vibrant coral reefs. The Bahamas offers excellent beginner sites with shallow, calm conditions, while **Bonaire in the Caribbean** is a diver's paradise with easy shore entries and protected marine parks. Other notable spots are the **Maldives, the Red Sea in Egypt, and the Florida Keys**. Each of these locations promises a unique underwater adventure, filled with colorful coral gardens, playful dolphins, and friendly sea turtles.

Investing in scuba gear can be a bit like shopping for a new wardrobe—exciting but overwhelming. The basic gear includes a mask, snorkel, fins, wetsuit, buoyancy control device (BCD), regulator, and tank. As a beginner, you might want to start by renting gear to get a feel for what you like. However, owning your equipment can be more comfortable and sanitary. When buying, focus on fit and comfort—nothing ruins a dive faster than an ill-fitting mask or a wetsuit that feels like a straitjacket. Maintenance is key to longevity; always rinse your gear with fresh water after dives and store it in a cool, dry place to prevent mold and damage.

Conservation awareness is a big part of diving responsibly. The underwater world is fragile, and it's our job to protect it. Always practice respectful diving by not touching or disturbing marine life and never collecting souvenirs. Participate in underwater clean-ups and spread the word about marine conservation. Educate yourself on the local ecosystems before each dive and choose operators committed to sustainable practices.

6.3 Motorcycle Road Trips: On the Open Road with Confidence

There's nothing quite like the thrill of the open road, the rushing wind, and the sense of freedom that comes with a motorcycle road trip. Whether you're cruising along scenic coastal highways or winding through rugged mountain passes, motorcycle travel offers a unique connection to the journey. It's not just about the destination, but the adventure of the ride itself—the ability to explore at your own pace, discover hidden gems off the beaten path, and experience the landscape in an entirely new way. For beginners, this section will guide you through the essentials of planning your first motorcycle road trip, from selecting the right bike to ensuring your safety and comfort on the road.

Before you hit the highways, select the right motorcycle. Think of it as choosing a dance partner; you want someone who moves with you effortlessly. Comfort, handling, and reliability are key. For long-distance touring, consider a touring bike like the **Honda Gold Wing**, known for its plush seats and smooth ride, or the **BMW R 1250 RT**, which offers excellent handling and advanced features. If you prefer something lighter, a cruiser like the **Harley-Davidson Softail** might be more your style. These bikes are designed for comfort over long distances, with ergonomic seating and ample storage for your gear.

Speaking of gear, let's talk about the essentials. A high-quality helmet is non-negotiable; it's your best defense against the unexpected. Full-face helmets offer the most protection, but if you prefer something less confining, modular helmets are a great compromise. Protective clothing is also a must—think sturdy jackets with armor, gloves, and boots that cover your ankles. Weather can be unpredictable, so pack gear for various conditions: a breathable rain suit, thermal layers for chilly mornings, and ventilated jackets for hot afternoons. Don't forget a basic repair kit, including tire repair tools, a multi-tool, and spare fuses. These can save the day if you encounter minor issues on the road.

Planning your route is where the adventure truly begins. Instead of focusing on the fastest way from point A to point B, look for scenic roads and interesting stops. For those new to road trips or looking for a leisurely experience, start with routes that offer scenic beauty without the stress of challenging driving conditions. **The Great River Road** along the Mississippi River is an excellent choice for beginners, providing beautiful river views and easy-to-navigate roads through quaint Midwestern towns. Another beginner-friendly option is **Route 66**, particularly the stretch between Chicago and St. Louis. This iconic road trip offers wide, well-maintained highways and charming roadside stops, making it perfect for those easing into long-distance travel. It is also a classic ride that delivers a taste of history and culture.

The **Pacific Coast Highway in California** offers stunning ocean views, while the **Blue Ridge Parkway in Virginia** winds through picturesque mountains. For a more rugged experience, consider the **Beartooth Highway in Montana and Wyoming**, which takes you through some of the most dramatic alpine landscapes in the U.S., or the **Tail of the Dragon in Tennessee**, famous for its 318 curves over 11 miles, making it a thrilling ride for experienced motorcyclists.

If you're up for an international adventure, the **Great Ocean Road in Australia** is a breathtaking ride along the coastline, offering iconic views of the Twelve Apostles. In Europe, the **Stelvio Pass in Italy** is one of the highest and most challenging roads in the Alps, perfect for those seeking adventure and incredible mountain vistas. **Canada's Icefields Parkway**, which connects Jasper and Banff National Parks, offers jaw-dropping views of glaciers, turquoise lakes, and wildlife.

Each route you take should include regular rest stops, not just for refueling but to stretch your legs and take in the sights. Points of interest, like national parks, historic landmarks, and quirky roadside attractions, add flavor to your trip, making each day a new adventure. Whether you prefer scenic coastal drives, mountainous terrain, or cultural explorations, choosing the right route will elevate your motorcycle road trip to an unforgettable experience.

Joining motorcycle clubs or groups can enrich your road-tripping experience. These communities are treasure troves of knowledge, offering tips and advice from seasoned riders. Clubs often organize group rides, providing a safe and social way to explore new routes. You'll find camaraderie and support, whether you're navigating a tricky mountain pass or just looking for the best diner in town. Plus, riding with a group adds an extra layer of safety, as there's always someone watching your back.

Popular groups like the **Harley Owners Group (H.O.G.)**, one of the largest motorcycle communities globally, offer local chapters that organize rides and events year-round. For women riders, groups like **Women on Wheels (WOW)** or the **Motor Maids** provide a welcoming community focused on empowering female motorcyclists. If you're looking for long-distance travel tips or global routes, **Adventure Riders** is an online forum and group for adventure touring enthusiasts. The **American Motorcyclist Association (AMA)** also connects riders through organized events, rides, and races across the U.S., while the **Iron Butt Association** caters to those interested in extreme long-distance riding. Whether you're riding with a large club or a small local group, these communities bring a new dimension to your motorcycle adventures. Gear up, plan your route, and get ready to experience the thrill of the open road in a whole new way! Are you ready?

6.4 Hot Air Balloon Rides: Seeing the World from Above

There's something truly magical about the serene silence of floating above the earth, with the landscape unfolding beneath you like a patchwork quilt. Hot air ballooning offers this breathtaking experience, where the world seems to slow down, and you feel completely at peace, drifting gently in the breeze.

For me, hot air ballooning holds an especially dear place in my heart. Over twenty-five years ago, my husband proposed to me at a beautiful balloon festival in Ontario, Canada. The sky was filled with vibrant colors as dozens of balloons took flight, creating a mesmerizing scene. As we floated above the rolling hills and forests, he got down on one knee—an unforgettable moment set against the backdrop of the sky and earth coming together. That magical day remains one of the most cherished memories of our lives.

Hot air ballooning is an experience that offers both adventure and tranquility. Whether you're looking for a romantic moment, or want to enjoy panoramic views from above, it's a journey you won't forget.

Choosing a reliable operator is crucial for a safe and enjoyable flight. Look for companies with strong safety records and certified pilots. Customer reviews can also provide insights into the experience. Operators with a good reputation will offer comprehensive safety briefings and well-maintained equipment. Certified pilots, often with thousands of hours of flying experience, ensure that you're in safe hands. They'll guide you through the process, from takeoff to landing, making sure you're comfortable and informed throughout the journey.

Before you take off, expect a brief orientation where you'll learn about the balloon, the basket, and safety protocols. The preparation includes inflating the balloon, which is a spectacle in itself. As you ascend, the noise from the burners fades, replaced by the gentle whisper of the wind. The ride typically lasts an hour, giving you ample time to soak in panoramic views.

Destinations like **Cappadocia in Turkey** offer surreal landscapes dotted with fairy chimneys, while the **Loire Valley in France** presents châteaux and vineyards. Other fantastic spots include the **Serengeti in Tanzania,** where you might spot wildlife below, and **Napa Valley in California**, with its rolling vineyards. You can also float above the ancient temples of **Bagan in Myanmar**, or experience the stunning red rock formations in **Sedona, Arizona**. The **Masai Mara in Kenya** offers the chance to see the Great Migration from the air, while **Queenstown in New Zealand** provides an unforgettable backdrop of snow-capped mountains and shimmering lakes. For a more unique experience, try drifting over the mesmerizing desert dunes in **Dubai,** where the vast, golden landscape stretches endlessly beneath you.

Weather plays a significant role in ballooning. Ideal conditions include clear skies and calm winds. The best times of year for ballooning are typically spring and fall when the weather is stable and temperatures are mild. However, Mother Nature can be unpredictable, so flexibility is key. Flights are often scheduled for early morning or late afternoon when winds are typically calmer. If the weather doesn't cooperate, rescheduling might be necessary. While this can be disappointing, it's essential for safety. Keep an eye on the forecast and stay in touch with your operator for updates.

To ensure a comfortable and enjoyable experience, consider a few accessibility and comfort tips. Dress in layers, as temperatures can vary from ground level to higher altitudes. Wear comfortable shoes, as you'll be standing for the duration of the flight. Bringing a camera is a must, but make sure it has a strap to keep it secure. If you have mobility concerns, discuss them with the operator beforehand. Many companies offer accommodations, such as sturdy baskets with doors for easier access. With these preparations, you can fully enjoy the breathtaking views and the unique sensation of floating peacefully above the world.

6.5 White Water Rafting: Riding the Waves of Adventure

Navigating the twists and turns of a roaring river, feeling the spray of water on your face as you paddle through surging rapids, is an experience like no other. White water rafting delivers an exhilarating rush of adrenaline while immersing you in the beauty of nature. Let's start with the basics. Understanding river classifications is key to a safe and enjoyable experience. Rivers are rated from Class I to Class V, with Class I being gentle, easy waters suitable for beginners, and Class V reserved for experts who thrive on intense, turbulent rapids.

If you're new to the sport, start with Class I or II rivers, such as the **Nantahala River in North Carolina** or the **Kicking Horse River in Canada**. The **Rogue River in Oregon** offers a mix of calm and exciting sections, making it perfect for a varied experience. For those looking to venture further, the **Soca River in Slovenia** provides stunning scenery and manageable rapids, while the **Rio Grande in Texas** offers a unique blend of natural beauty and adventure.

The **Chattooga River** on the border of **Georgia and South Carolina** is another great option for beginners, with sections offering both peaceful paddling and thrilling rapids. The **Lower New River in West Virginia** also features calm stretches that are ideal for newcomers to whitewater rafting.

The **Snake River in Wyoming** offers scenic Class I and II sections through Grand Teton National Park, where you can enjoy wildlife sightings and incredible mountain views. The **Middle Fork of the American River in California** is another great option for beginners, with plenty of gentle rapids and stunning canyon landscapes.

For more experienced rafters, **the Colorado River through the Grand Canyon** delivers an epic adventure, offering a combination of heart-pounding Class IV and V rapids along with jaw-dropping canyon views. **Costa Rica's Pacuare River** is a must-visit for those seeking both thrilling rapids and lush, tropical surroundings, often touted as one of the most beautiful rivers in the world. The **Zambezi River in Zambia,** with its world-class Class V rapids near Victoria Falls, and the **Futaleufú River in Chile**, set against the dramatic Patagonian landscape, are also prime destinations for seasoned adventurers. For an exotic experience, consider the **Ayung River in Bali**, where you'll navigate rapids while surrounded by vibrant jungles and ancient temples.

Safety and training are non-negotiable when it comes to white water rafting. Always go with guided tours led by professional rafting companies. These experts provide not just the equipment but also the knowledge and skills to ensure a safe trip. Before you even dip a toe in the water, you'll receive a safety briefing covering everything from paddling techniques to what to do if you fall in. Experienced guides lead the way, directing the raft and ensuring everyone works together. They keep a vigilant eye on the river's conditions, adjusting the plan as needed to keep you safe. Remember, the best adventures are those you can relive with joy, not regret.

White water rafting demands a good level of physical fitness and a willingness to work as a team. Paddling through rapids requires strength and coordination, and you'll need to follow the guide's commands precisely to navigate the river successfully. This isn't just a solo endeavor; teamwork is crucial. Each person in the raft plays a vital role, whether it's paddling in sync or leaning the right way to balance the raft. Think of it as a group dance, where everyone's movements must align. It's a fantastic way to bond with friends or family, turning a thrilling adventure into a shared triumph.

While you're having the time of your life, it's important to remember that these waterways are delicate ecosystems. Promoting environmental awareness is part of the adventure. Follow 'Leave No Trace' principles—pack out everything you bring in and avoid disturbing wildlife. Participate in river clean-up initiatives if you can. Many rafting companies support these efforts and welcome volunteers. By respecting the natural beauty of these rivers, you ensure they remain pristine for future adventurers. Think of it as giving back to the places that give you so much joy.

6.6 Mountain Biking for the Energetic Retiree

The thrill of riding through lush forests, over rolling hills, and along scenic trails, all while getting a fantastic workout, is what makes mountain biking so appealing. It's not just for the young and reckless; it's a fantastic fit for retirees looking to add a dash of adventure to their fitness routine. This sport combines cardiovascular exercise, strength training, and mental challenges, making it a triple benefit to your health. Pedaling up hills gets your heart pumping, navigating rocky paths improves your balance and coordination, and the sheer joy of being outdoors boosts your mental well-being. It's like a gym session, a nature hike, and a meditation retreat all rolled into one.

While I'm not into mountain biking myself, my husband is an avid mountain biker and has explored some of the most scenic and challenging trails out there. He's tackled routes in places like **Mont-Sainte-Anne in Quebec, Canada** - the home to the UCI Mountain Bike World Cup, **Cortina d'Ampezzo in Italy, Mount Snow in Vermont**, and the epic **Continental Divide Trail in Colorado**, to name a few. While I usually hike during his rides, through his adventures, I've come to appreciate the beauty and excitement that mountain biking offers. For those seeking an adventurous way to stay fit, it's hard to beat the thrill of the ride.

Choosing the right equipment is crucial for a safe and enjoyable mountain biking experience. Start with the bike itself. Look for a model that offers good suspension to absorb shocks and a comfortable seat to save your backside on long rides. Brands like **Trek, Specialized, and Giant** offer excellent options tailored for all skill levels. A well-fitting helmet is your first line of defense, and don't skimp on quality. Pads for your knees and elbows can save you from scrapes and bruises. Consider investing in a good pair of gloves to improve your grip and reduce hand fatigue. A hydration pack, like a CamelBak, ensures you stay hydrated without having to stop frequently. Additional equipment like a small first aid kit, a multi-tool for quick repairs, and a portable pump can make your rides more enjoyable and trouble-free.

Starting safely with mountain biking involves easing into the sport. Don't rush to tackle the most challenging trails right away. Begin with flat, easy trails to build your confidence and skills. Learn to read trail ratings, which indicate the difficulty level. Green trails are beginner-friendly, blue are intermediate, and black diamond trails are for advanced riders. Stick to green trails initially, focusing on basic skills like shifting gears, braking, and maintaining balance. Gradual skill-building is essential. As you get more comfortable, try trails with slight inclines and gentle descents. Remember, it's not about speed; it's about enjoying the ride and staying safe.

British Columbia, where we live, is home to some of the world's best mountain biking destinations. **Whistler** is a globally renowned hotspot with trails for all levels, while **Vancouver's North Shore** offers excellent beginner and intermediate paths. Don't miss **Silver Star Mountain in Vernon**, BC, known for its variety of trails and breathtaking views. In the U.S., iconic spots like **Moab, Utah**, provide stunning red rock landscapes, while **Sedona, Arizona**, features scenic desert routes. For lush, forested adventures, **Pisgah National Forest in North Carolina** is a great option.

In Europe, **Cortina d'Ampezzo in Italy** delivers stunning rides through the Dolomites, and **Les Gets in France** is a favorite for alpine biking. **Austria's Saalbach-Hinterglemm** offers an extensive network of trails with views of the Austrian Alps. In **Spain, the Pyrenees** offer challenging trails with rewarding views, while **Slovenia's** bike parks, especially in **Kranjska Gora**, provide both thrilling descents and beautiful alpine scenery.

Joining mountain biking clubs or community groups can enhance your experience. These clubs offer structured rides, providing a safe environment for beginners to learn. They often organize group rides, where experienced riders share tips and advice. This camaraderie makes the sport more enjoyable and helps you push your limits safely. Clubs also offer social events, workshops, and even trips to famous biking trails. Whether you're a solo rider looking to make new friends or someone who enjoys group activities, these communities can provide the support and motivation you need to keep riding.

6.7 Soaring Through the Skies with Zip-Lining

Zip-lining is one of those heart-pumping adventures that can make you feel like a kid again, no matter your age. Gliding through the treetops or across expansive valleys, feeling the wind in your face as you speed through the air, is a thrilling experience that gives you a unique perspective of nature. Best of all, zip-lining can be a fantastic option for retirees looking for an adventurous activity that's both exhilarating and accessible.

Safety is always the top priority, and the good news is that zip-lining is designed with rigorous safety protocols in place. Reputable zip-lining companies provide professional guides who ensure that you're harnessed securely and thoroughly briefed on how to zip-line safely. The equipment used—harnesses, helmets, carabiners, and zip-line cables—undergoes regular safety checks to meet industry standards. Always choose zip-lining operators who are certified by recognized safety organizations, such as the **Association for Challenge Course Technology (ACCT)** or other local governing bodies. Don't hesitate to ask questions about the safety record of the company before booking, and look for glowing reviews from other participants.

Zip-lining doesn't require extensive physical training, but it's important to ensure you're comfortable with the idea of heights and short bursts of physical activity. Some courses involve hiking between zip lines, so a moderate level of fitness is recommended. Be sure to dress appropriately—closed-toe shoes with a good grip are essential, and wearing comfortable, weather-appropriate clothing will keep you at ease during the experience. If you have any health concerns, such as heart conditions or mobility limitations, check with your doctor beforehand to ensure zip-lining is safe for you.

The beauty of zip-lining is that it can be found in some of the world's most scenic destinations. In the U.S., **Haleakalā National Park in Maui, Hawaii,** offers an unforgettable zip-lining experience where you can glide over lush forests with views of volcanic craters. The **Great Smoky Mountains in Tennessee and North Carolina** feature treetop zip-line courses with incredible views of the rolling mountains and valleys below. **Hunter Mountain in New York's Catskills** region offers a long and thrilling zip-line ride that's perfect for adventure-seekers of all ages.

For those looking to explore beyond the U.S., **Costa Rica** is a zip-lining paradise, with courses through the dense canopies of tropical rainforests, where you might spot exotic wildlife from above. The **Arenal Volcano** area, in particular, is known for its breathtaking zip-lining tours over waterfalls and lush greenery. In Canada, **Whistler in British Columbia** is famous for its stunning zip-lining courses that allow you to soar over alpine forests and crystal-clear lakes. Europe has its own share of thrills, with **Interlaken in Switzerland** offering scenic zip-lining experiences through the majestic Swiss Alps, and **Madeira, Portugal,** providing coastal and mountainous views as you zip through nature reserves.

One of the best things about zip-lining is its accessibility. It's not an overly physically demanding activity, making it suitable for retirees who want an adventurous experience without the intensity of high-impact sports. Plus, zip-lining companies usually cater to all fitness levels, and guides are always on hand to ensure you feel safe and comfortable. Whether you're zipping through a forest canopy or across a mountain range, the thrill is unforgettable, but so is the sense of accomplishment. It's an exciting, yet manageable, adventure that leaves you feeling energized and connected to the great outdoors.

As with any adventure, don't forget to capture the memories. Many zip-lining companies offer helmet-mounted GoPro rentals or photo packages that document your entire experience. Whether it's the breathtaking landscapes or the joy on your face, these memories will be ones to cherish for years to come.

Adventure is the spice of life, and your golden years are the perfect time to savor it. From thrilling skydives to serene hot-air balloon rides, to heart-pounding white-water rafting, the opportunities for excitement are endless.

As we descend from the thrilling heights of skydiving and the depths of scuba diving, it's time to reconnect with the serenity of nature in all its beauty. For those who find joy in quieter, yet equally rewarding pursuits, the great outdoors offers endless possibilities. In the next chapter, we'll explore how to fully embrace the outdoors, offering activities that blend excitement with the calming presence of nature.

7

The Great Outdoors: Exploring Nature's Wonders

The beauty of the natural world is that it caters to everyone as outdoor activities provide a space for reflection, physical fitness, and a little adventure. There's something truly special about stepping outside and feeling the gentle warmth of the sun or the cool shade of a forest canopy. Whether you're strolling through a quiet woodland trail, exploring scenic mountain paths, or simply sitting by a tranquil lake, nature has a way of grounding us and reminding us of life's simple pleasures. Spending time outdoors is not just a pastime—it's a chance to reconnect with the world around us, stay active, and find joy in exploration.

7.1 Bird-Watching: Connecting with Nature's Winged Wonders

Bird-watching opens up a world of quiet excitement and connection with nature. From the delicate flutter of a hummingbird to the graceful glide of an eagle, each moment spent observing birds is an opportunity to witness the beauty of the natural world. The thrill lies in the unpredictability—whether you're in your own backyard or exploring a nature reserve, you never know which species will cross your path.

Bird-watching is not only a relaxing and fulfilling pastime but also a chance to sharpen your observation skills, stay active, and appreciate the wonders of nature. It's a perfect way to enjoy the outdoors while engaging in a lifelong learning experience.

Choosing the right equipment is the first step in becoming a bird-watching aficionado. You don't need to break the bank to get started, but a good pair of binoculars can make all the difference. Look for binoculars with a magnification of 8x or 10x and ensure they are lightweight and easy to handle. Brands like **Nikon** and **Bushnell** offer reliable options at various price points. A field guide is also essential; it's the birdwatcher's bible. Guides like the **Sibley Field Guide to Birds**, the **Peterson Field Guide to Birds of North America**, and **The Golden Guide's Birds of North America**, which is portable and accessible for beginners, are excellent choices. These books offer detailed illustrations and descriptions, making it easier to identify the feathered friends you encounter.

Best bird-watching practices are crucial for a rewarding experience. Start by choosing the best times of day for bird-watching, typically early morning or late afternoon when birds are most active. Remain quiet and unobtrusive; sudden movements or loud noises easily startle birds. Wear neutral-colored clothing to blend into the environment. Learn to use your binoculars efficiently by practicing at home, focusing on stationary objects before moving targets. The more you practice, the better you'll become at spotting and identifying birds. Familiarize yourself with common species in your area, and gradually expand your knowledge to include rarer finds. Websites like **eBird** can be invaluable for tracking bird sightings and learning about local species.

Local bird-watching spots can turn an ordinary day into an extraordinary adventure. National parks and nature reserves are often teeming with bird life. Places like the **Everglades National Park in Florida** or **Point Reyes National Seashore in California** are renowned for their avian diversity. Even local parks and green spaces can be treasure troves of bird activity. Many nature reserves offer guided bird-watching tours tailored to seniors, providing an opportunity to learn from experienced guides and meet fellow bird enthusiasts. These tours often reveal hidden gems and secret spots that you might miss on your own.

In addition to these U.S. hotspots, you can find other incredible destinations for bird-watching around the world. The **Amazon Rainforest in Brazil** offers the chance to spot hundreds of exotic species, including colorful toucans and macaws. In Europe, the wetlands of **Doñana National Park in Spain** provide a haven for flamingos and other migratory birds. If you're seeking something more remote, **New Zealand's Stewart Island** is home to rare species like the kiwi and yellow-eyed penguin. **Canada's Point Pelee National Park in Ontario** is famous for its spring migration, attracting bird enthusiasts from around the globe. **In Africa, the Okavango Delta in Botswana** offers an unparalleled bird-watching experience, with species like the African fish eagle soaring above its pristine waters.

Join bird-watching clubs to enrich your experience and enhance your skills. Local clubs provide a platform to meet fellow enthusiasts, exchange information, and take part in organized outings. Clubs often host events like bird counts, workshops, and lectures, offering both social and educational benefits. Websites like **Audubon** or **BirdingPal** can help you find clubs in your area.

Always take a moment to reflect on your bird-watching journey. What are your favorite bird-watching spots? Have you had any memorable encounters with rare birds? How has bird-watching enriched your connection with nature? Jot down your thoughts and experiences in a journal. This reflection can deepen your appreciation for this delightful pastime and inspire new adventures in the great outdoors.

7.2 Fishing and Boating: Relaxing by the Water

Imagine casting a line into a serene lake, the sun gently warming your back, and the anticipation of that first bite. Getting started with fishing is easier than you might think. Freshwater fishing is perfect for beginners, whether you're at a local pond or a lazy river. A simple rod and reel combo, a tackle box with hooks, weights, and a variety of bait can get you started. If you prefer the thrill of the ocean, saltwater fishing might be your calling. Here, you'll need sturdier gear to handle bigger fish and the salty environment. Fly-fishing, on the other hand, is an art form of gracefully casting a delicate fly to land just right in a stream, enticing a trout. It requires a bit more finesse and specialized equipment like a fly rod, reel, and flies that mimic insects.

Safety on the water is paramount, especially as we get older. Always wear a life jacket. It's not just a safety precaution—it's literally a lifesaver. Understanding boat operation basics is crucial too. If you're new to boating, consider taking a boating safety course. These courses cover everything from navigation rules to emergency procedures. Knowing local boating laws and regulations can save you from fines and ensure a safe outing. For instance, some areas require specific permits or have speed limits to protect wildlife and other boaters. Make sure your boat is equipped with safety gear like flares, a first-aid kit, and a whistle. And remember, never boat alone—having a buddy ensures someone's there to help if something goes wrong.

Finding accessible fishing and boating locations that cater to seniors can make your experience even more enjoyable. Look for places with amenities like piers, ramps, and rental facilities that offer senior assistance. State parks often have accessible fishing spots with flat, stable surfaces and handrails. Marinas sometimes offer boat rentals with easy boarding options and staff to assist you. For example, **Lake Tahoe** has several marinas that rent out boats and provide assistance to ensure a smooth and enjoyable day on the water. The **Florida Keys** offer many fishing charters that cater to seniors, providing everything from equipment to bait.

Local fishing clubs are fantastic for learning from more experienced anglers. These clubs often organize group fishing trips, providing a chance to explore new spots and techniques. It's also a great way to make new friends who share your passion. Clubs often host events, workshops, and tournaments, making it easy to stay engaged and motivated. Websites like **Meetup** and local community boards are good places to find these clubs.

7.3 Exploring the Wonders of National Parks

There's something awe-inspiring about stepping into a national park, where the beauty of nature stretches as far as the eye can see and history is etched into every landscape. Whether you're gazing over the vast expanse of the Grand Canyon, walking beneath towering redwoods, or listening to the gentle rustle of leaves in the breeze, national parks offer a unique opportunity to reconnect with the natural world. These protected spaces are not just for the adventurous—they provide a sanctuary for retirees seeking both tranquility and adventure. From accessible trails to educational programs, exploring national parks can turn your retirement years into a journey of discovery, filled with breathtaking views, wildlife encounters, and moments of quiet reflection in nature's grandest settings.

Selecting the right national park can elevate your retirement adventures to new heights. Look for parks that are senior-friendly, with accessible trails, well-equipped visitor centers, and educational programs. **Yellowstone National Park** offers stunning geysers and wildlife viewing, with accessible boardwalks and shuttle services. **Acadia National Park in Maine** provides beautiful coastal views and wheelchair-accessible trails like the Ocean Path. Other notable mentions include **Zion National Park** with its easily navigable Pa'rus Trail, and the **Everglades National Park**, where you can explore the unique ecosystem via accessible trails and boat tours. Don't overlook the **Great Smoky Mountains, Shenandoah National Park, or the Blue Ridge Parkway**, all of which offer a mix of accessibility and breathtaking scenery.

My husband and I have had some unforgettable experiences exploring many of these majestic parks, and our visits have been nothing short of incredible. From the jaw-dropping vistas of **Yosemite's** granite cliffs to the deep blue waters of **Crater Lake**, each destination offered its own unique charm. **Canyonlands** took us into a desert wonderland of rock formations where gods got really serious about architecture and design. And **Olympic National Park** treated us to a blend of lush rainforests and rugged coastlines. Each park gave us the chance to immerse ourselves in nature's beauty, leaving us with treasured memories of adventure and awe.

Maximizing park benefits extends beyond just the physical experience. Research has shown that spending time in nature can significantly boost your mental well-being, lower stress levels, and even improve your immune system. Participating in ranger-led tours and nature workshops can deepen your appreciation for these natural wonders. Imagine learning about the geology of the Grand Canyon from an expert or understanding the delicate ecosystems of the Everglades through a hands-on workshop. These programs not only educate but also provide opportunities to meet fellow nature enthusiasts and make new friends. The psychological benefits of immersing yourself in nature are profound, offering a sense of peace and fulfillment that's hard to replicate elsewhere.

Safety and accessibility features are crucial for ensuring a comfortable and enjoyable experience. Many parks offer shuttle services that can take you to key viewpoints and trailheads, reducing the need for extensive walking. Accessible trail ratings help you choose paths that match your fitness level and mobility. Accommodations within or near the parks often provide accessible rooms equipped with features like grab bars in the bathrooms, roll-in showers, and wider doorways. For instance, **Yosemite National Park** has accommodations ranging from accessible campsites to fully equipped lodges. Always check the park's website or contact the visitor center for up-to-date information on accessibility features and safety guidelines.

Conservation and etiquette play a significant role in preserving these natural treasures for future generations. Simple practices like packing out all your trash, staying on designated trails, and respecting wildlife can make a big difference. Many parks have volunteer programs where you can contribute to conservation efforts, such as trail maintenance or habitat restoration. Seniors often bring a wealth of knowledge and experience to these initiatives, making them invaluable advocates for conservation. Imagine the satisfaction of knowing you've played a part in preserving the beauty of Yellowstone or the biodiversity of the Everglades. Your efforts ensure these parks remain pristine and accessible for years to come, allowing future generations to enjoy the same breathtaking landscapes and experiences.

7.4 Hidden Treasures: The Exciting World of Treasure Hunting

The thrill of a treasure hunt combined with the joy of exploring new places. That's geocaching—a real-world, outdoor adventure game that uses GPS-enabled devices to find hidden containers, or "caches," scattered around the world. It's like a modern-day treasure hunt, perfect for adding a dash of excitement to your retirement. Each cache contains a logbook to sign and sometimes trinkets to trade. The beauty of geocaching is that it can be done anywhere, from your local park to exotic destinations, making it an ideal hobby for both homebodies and globetrotters alike.

To get started, you'll need to set up a geocaching account. Head over to the **Geocaching.com** website or download the app on your smartphone. Sign up for a free account, though premium memberships offer additional features. Once you're logged in, you can search for caches nearby. Caches are rated by difficulty and terrain, so choose one that matches your comfort level. The app provides coordinates and clues to guide you. Input the coordinates into your GPS device or use your smartphone's built-in GPS to start your hunt. It's that simple! Just think of it as a high-tech scavenger hunt that takes you to interesting nooks and crannies you might never have discovered otherwise.

The health benefits of geocaching are a fantastic bonus. This activity encourages walking and mild physical exertion, which can improve cardiovascular health and overall fitness. Navigating to caches also involves a bit of problem-solving and mental stimulation, keeping your brain engaged. The excitement of finding a cache can be a great motivator for spending time outdoors and exploring new locations. Imagine the joy of discovering a hidden gem in your neighborhood or stumbling upon a breathtaking view you never knew existed. It's a fun way to stay active and curious, turning every outing into an adventure.

While on your geocaching quests, it's important to follow some basic etiquette and safety rules. Always leave the cache as you found it, ensuring it's well-hidden for the next adventurer. Respect the environment—don't disturb plants or wildlife, and stick to marked paths. Carry a small bag to pick up any litter you come across; it's a small act that contributes to the beauty and cleanliness of the area. Safety-wise, always let someone know where you're going and when you expect to return, especially if you're venturing into remote areas. Wear appropriate clothing and footwear for the terrain, and bring essentials like water, snacks, and a first-aid kit. With these precautions, you can enjoy the thrill of the hunt safely and responsibly.

7.5 Camping and Glamping: Relaxing Outdoor Retreats

Camping is a fantastic way to immerse yourself in nature, with the crackle of a campfire, the scent of pine trees, and the starry sky above. But let's be honest—not everyone is thrilled at the idea of sleeping on an air mattress or braving the elements. This is where glamping, or glamorous camping, comes in. Traditional camping involves pitching a tent, cooking over an open fire, and sleeping on a sleeping mat. It's rugged and adventurous. Glamping, on the other hand, offers the same connection with nature but with a touch of luxury. Think cozy tents with proper beds, gourmet meals, kitchenettes, and private bathrooms. If you love the idea of being outdoors but crave comfort, glamping might just be your perfect match.

When it comes to gear, both camping and glamping require some preparation. For traditional camping, invest in a high-quality tent that's easy to set up and offers good ventilation. Comfortable sleeping mats or air mattresses are a must; your back will thank you. Ergonomic chairs can make sitting around the campfire more enjoyable. Don't forget a reliable cooler to keep your food fresh and a portable stove for cooking.

Glamping requires less gear than traditional camping, but it's always worth adding personal touches like soft blankets, fairy lights for ambiance, and perhaps a portable fan or heater depending on the season. However, before packing, it's important to check what is provided by the glamping facility. Some glam sites offer nearly everything, from towels and toiletries to cooking equipment, while others may require you to bring essentials like towels, a first aid kit, insect repellent, or even pots and pans. Cutlery, dishes, and cooking utensils might also be necessary depending on the site, so it's always a good idea to confirm what's included ahead of time. Having the right gear can make all the difference in ensuring a comfortable and enjoyable experience, whether you're roughing it or indulging in a luxurious stay.

Finding senior-friendly campgrounds can enhance your outdoor experience. Look for campgrounds that offer easy access to medical facilities. Many state parks and private campgrounds cater to seniors, providing level campsites with easy access to facilities. Some even offer cabins, yurts, safari-style lodges, and treehouses for those who prefer a bit more comfort or adventure. Websites like **Recreation.gov** and **KOA** can help you find campgrounds with the amenities you need. These sites often feature reviews from other campers, so you can get an idea of what to expect before you go, such as clean restrooms and hot showers.

Activities in campgrounds are varied and can be tailored to your interests and energy levels. Nature walks are a fantastic way to explore your surroundings; many campgrounds have well-marked trails that range from easy to challenging. Photography can capture the beauty of your adventure, whether it's a stunning sunrise or a curious squirrel. Relaxing in nature, reading a book, or listening to the sounds of the forest can be incredibly rejuvenating. Safety should always be a priority. Always inform someone of your plans, carry a first-aid kit, and be aware of local wildlife. Make sure your campsite is free of food scraps to avoid attracting animals. And always follow fire safety guidelines if you're enjoying a campfire.

7.6 Charting the Course: Planning Your Dream RV Adventure

There's nothing quite like the freedom of hitting the open road in an RV, where your home travels with you, offering the flexibility to explore new destinations at your own pace. Whether you're parked by a serene lake, nestled in a forest, or overlooking a breathtaking mountain range, the possibilities for adventure and discovery are endless. RV travel allows you to embrace spontaneity, wake up to a new view each morning, and enjoy the comforts of home wherever you go.

Choosing the right RV is crucial for comfort and ease. For retirees, think about a Class B or C motorhome. These are smaller and more maneuverable compared to the larger Class A rigs, making them perfect for navigating both highways and scenic byways. Look for features that prioritize comfort, such as a spacious sleeping area, a well-equipped kitchen, and a bathroom with a decent-sized shower. Maintenance shouldn't be a headache, so opt for models known for reliability and ease of upkeep. Brands like **Winnebago** and **Airstream** are often praised for their quality and durability.

Mapping out your journey is where the fun begins. Picture cruising along the **Pacific Coast Highway** with the ocean on one side and towering cliffs on the other. Or perhaps winding through the **Blue Ridge Parkway,** surrounded by the vibrant hues of autumn leaves. When planning your route, consider destinations that offer both scenic beauty and accessibility. National parks like **Yellowstone, Acadia**, and the **Grand Canyon** are fantastic choices, with plenty of RV-friendly facilities. The **Outer Banks in North Carolina** or **Florida's Everglades National Park** also make for memorable stops, blending natural beauty with accessible campgrounds. Canada offers stunning options, like **Banff and Jasper National Parks in Alberta**, where you can park your RV amid towering peaks and turquoise lakes. For a coastal adventure, head to the **Cabot Trail in Nova Scotia**, where you can drive along dramatic cliffs, explore quaint fishing villages, and camp with breathtaking ocean views. In **British Columbia, Vancouver Island's Pacific Rim National Park Reserve** offers lush rainforests, sandy beaches, and endless opportunities for wildlife spotting right from your RV. For a more remote experience, venture to **Gros Morne National Park in Newfoundland,** where the rugged landscape and fjords create a true sense of wilderness adventure. **Ontario's Algonquin Provincial Park** offers serene lakes and endless opportunities for wildlife viewing.

Apps like **RV Parky** or **AllStays** can help you find campgrounds, rest stops, and points of interest along the way. Don't forget to include some quirky stops, like the world's largest ball of twine or a local food festival. Consider visiting odd roadside attractions like the **Cadillac Ranch in Texas**, where vintage cars are half-buried in the desert, or the giant **Paul Bunyan statue in Minnesota.** For a touch of nostalgia, stop by classic diners or vintage gas stations along **Route 66**. You could even visit niche museums, like the **Spam Museum in Minnesota** or the **UFO Museum in Roswell, New Mexico.** Seeking something unique? How about checking out the colorful street art of **Wynwood Walls in Miami** or the **Enchanted Highway in North Dakota**, where oversized metal sculptures dot the landscape? Each quirky stop adds character to your journey and creates memories that go beyond the typical travel itinerary.

Safety and maintenance are non-negotiable for a worry-free trip. Before hitting the road, conduct a thorough pre-trip inspection. Check tire pressure, fluid levels, and ensure all lights are functioning. Make a checklist to cover everything from securing loose items inside the RV to testing the brakes. Keep a basic toolkit and spare parts handy; you never know when you might need to tighten a bolt or replace a fuse. Safety extends to driving practices as well. Take your time, especially on unfamiliar roads, and always be mindful of the RV's size, especially when maneuvering through tight spaces or parking.

Community and resources can elevate your RV experience. Joining RV clubs like the **Good Sam Club** or **Escapees RV Club** connects you with a network of fellow enthusiasts who share tips, advice, and stories. Online forums and social media groups are treasure troves of information, from the best campgrounds, to the ones you need to avoid, to must-see hidden gems. These communities offer support and camaraderie, turning solo adventures into shared experiences.

7.7 Horseback Riding: Essentials for a Safe and Enjoyable Experience

Horseback riding is a timeless activity that offers a unique way to enjoy the outdoors while staying active. Whether you're trotting through open meadows, winding along forest trails, or taking in the serene beauty of a mountain vista, horseback riding combines adventure, relaxation, and a connection to nature. Beyond the sheer joy of it, riding a horse improves your balance and core strength. As you adjust to the horse's movements, your muscles engage in a workout that's both gentle and effective. It's like having a fitness class in nature. And let's not forget the stress reduction. There's something incredibly soothing about the steady, rhythmic motion of horseback riding. It's a perfect way to clear your mind and find a sense of calm amidst life's hustle and bustle.

Selecting a riding school that caters to beginners, particularly older adults, is crucial for a safe and enjoyable experience. Look for schools that provide gentle, well-trained horses. These horses are usually calm and accustomed to novice riders, making them the perfect companions for your equestrian adventure. Ask about the instructors' qualifications and experience with older riders. A good instructor will be patient, understanding, and capable of teaching at a pace that suits you. Visit the school beforehand to get a feel for the environment and the horses.

Safety gear and techniques are top priorities for horseback riding. Always wear a helmet; it's your first line of defense against head injuries. Proper footwear is also important—opt for boots with a small heel to prevent your feet from slipping through the stirrups. Comfortable, breathable clothing that allows freedom of movement is ideal.

Learning basic riding techniques can enhance your experience and safety. Start with mastering the mounting and dismounting process. Learn how to hold the reins, guide the horse, and use basic commands like "walk," "trot," and "stop." Understanding these fundamentals can boost your confidence and ensure a smoother ride.

One of the most rewarding aspects of horseback riding is the connection with nature. Riding through a forest trail or across a meadow provides a unique perspective on the natural world. You're not just observing nature; you're a part of it. The horse becomes your guide, leading you through landscapes you might never have explored on foot. This connection with nature is invigorating and tranquil at the same time. But equally special is the bond you form with the horse itself. Horses, with their gentle strength, grace, and intelligence, have a way of sensing their rider's emotions and adapting accordingly. As you ride, you develop a sense of trust and communication with your horse, working together to navigate the terrain. It's a partnership that brings a deeper level of awareness and connection to your surroundings. The horse's beauty, with its flowing mane and powerful, elegant stride, adds to the experience, making it not just a physical journey but an emotional one as well. Whether you're riding along a beach, through a mountain trail, or in a serene park, the experience is bound to leave you refreshed and rejuvenated, both from the beauty of nature and the unique bond with your horse.

7.8. Exploring the Night Sky: Stargazing and Astronomy Clubs

I think everyone agrees that there's something absolutely magical about standing under a clear night sky, with the stars twinkling above you, far from the hustle and bustle of everyday life. For people looking to reconnect with nature and find a sense of awe in the great outdoors, stargazing offers the perfect escape. It's a peaceful yet invigorating activity that you can enjoy from your own backyard or while traveling to some of the world's best dark-sky locations. The beauty of this hobby is that you can start simple—no need for a telescope just yet. Begin by learning to identify some of the major constellations, such as Orion, Ursa Major, and Cassiopeia. Apps like **SkyView** or **Star Walk** can help guide you as you explore the night sky, pointing out planets, stars, and constellations as you go. All you need is a comfortable chair, a blanket, and a clear night.

Once you're hooked, you might want to invest in a telescope for a closer look at the planets, moons, and star clusters that fill the night sky. Telescopes range from beginner-friendly models to more advanced equipment, so start with one that fits your needs. For beginners, a simple refractor telescope with a 60-80mm aperture is a great starting point. This type of telescope is easy to use and portable, making it ideal for casual stargazing. If you're more serious about the hobby, consider a Dobsonian or reflector telescope, which provides more power and allows you to see deep-sky objects like galaxies, nebulae, and distant planets. Don't forget about essential accessories, such as a star map and a red flashlight (which helps preserve your night vision). Binoculars are also a great alternative for beginners and are portable for easy stargazing on the go. Look for features such as adjustable magnification, sturdy tripods, and portability if you plan to take your stargazing adventures to remote locations.

One of the best ways to deepen your appreciation of the night sky is by joining an astronomy club. These groups often organize star-gazing events, where members gather in open areas away from city lights for the best views. Sharing the experience with others can make it even more enjoyable, and experienced astronomers are always happy to share their knowledge and equipment. Whether you're spotting a shooting star or marveling at a lunar eclipse, an astronomy club offers a great way to meet like-minded people and discover new celestial wonders.

Stargazing is about more than just looking up—it's about immersing yourself in nature and appreciating the tranquility of the great outdoors. You may stargaze from a remote mountain lodge, a national park, or even during a camping trip under a vast, starry sky. Many national parks, such as **Bryce Canyon** and **Big Bend** in the **U.S.**, or **Jasper National Park in Canada**, offer designated dark sky preserves, making them perfect for stargazing enthusiasts. As the sun sets and the stars emerge, you'll find stargazing to be a meditative outdoor activity, helping you to slow down, breathe deeply, and reconnect with nature in a peaceful, awe-inspiring way.

The outdoor element of astronomy adds a whole new dimension to this activity. Whether you're attending a stargazing event at a nearby observatory or camping under the stars in a remote wilderness area, this hobby lets you explore the world in a different light—literally. You might plan trips to renowned dark sky reserves or attend stargazing festivals, combining travel with your new passion for the night sky.

Please refer to the **Resources Chapter** for a list of some popular stargazing festivals.

The connection between the beauty of the cosmos and the great outdoors makes stargazing an enriching adventure for your retirement years.

As we wrap up this chapter on the Great Outdoors, it's clear that nature offers endless opportunities for joy, adventure, and connection. Whether you're bird-watching, hiking, fishing, or horseback riding, each activity brings its own unique benefits.

8
Conclusion

So here we are, at the end of this book and at the beginning of your journey. Remember that moment when I realized retirement wasn't just some distant concept, but a reality staring me in the face? Friends around me were retiring, and I thought, "Hey, I want to retire—but what then?" That moment of clarity sent me on a deep dive into exploring what retirement could be—a phase of life filled with opportunities, growth, and excitement. This book was born from that journey, designed to help you embrace retirement with confidence and enthusiasm.

We've covered a wide range of exciting possibilities together. From the importance of health and fitness in keeping your body and mind sharp, to planning unforgettable travel adventures that span serene outdoor escapes, cultural tours through Europe, and adrenaline-pumping sports like skydiving and scuba diving. Whether you're hiking through national parks, bird-watching in scenic reserves, or exploring ancient ruins in far-off lands, the aim has been to inspire you to fully embrace life in retirement, pursuing activities that fuel both your passion and your well-being. We've explored how to maximize these exciting experiences while staying mindful of your health, safety, and budget. You've seen that you can fill your retirement years with travel, excitement, and wellness without sacrificing financial peace of mind.

The key takeaway? Stay open to new experiences, prioritize health and wellness, and remember that this chapter of your life is a thrilling new beginning. It's a time to explore fun, adventure, and personal growth like never before.

Now, here's your call to action: pick at least one new activity or destination that excites you and start planning for it. Trust me, stepping out of your comfort zone will be the best decision you make. Whether it's booking that river cruise you've always dreamed of, or simply taking a leisurely walk through a local nature trail, every small step counts.

Reflecting on my own journey, I've seen firsthand how these activities can transform your life into a richer, more fulfilling experience. I'm confident that with the right mindset, your retirement years can truly be your best years yet.

Share Your Adventure and Inspire Others

As you reach the end of *The Great Retirement Escape*, I hope this book has fueled your enthusiasm for the adventures and experiences that await. Whether it's a scenic road trip, a thrilling new sport, or a leisurely escape to a hidden gem, retirement is an open invitation to explore the world on your terms.

If this book has inspired you or helped shape your retirement plans, I'd love if you leave a review! Your review could help others discover the possibilities in their retirement journeys and can guide those who are ready to make retirement their most adventurous chapter yet. A few sentences are all it takes, but feel free to share as much as you'd like about what you found useful or inspiring.

Thank you. Your support as a reader is deeply appreciated, and your experience could be the nudge someone else needs to begin their retirement adventure. Here's to making retirement everything you've dreamed of—and much, much more!

About the Author

Lara West is a health and wellness advocate dedicated to empowering readers through her insightful writings. With a particular emphasis on women's and midlife health, Lara shares relatable and practical tips drawn from her personal experiences that deeply resonate with her readers.

Her journey began in her mid-forties as she faced perimenopausal symptoms, leaky gut syndrome, an autoimmune disease, and the challenges of caregiving for a family member with dementia. This transformative period ignited her passion for understanding gut health and its significant impact on overall well-being, as well as the importance of self-care for caregivers.

Lara's commitment to holistic wellness inspires her to share practical strategies for navigating the challenges of middle age, caregiving, and maintaining an active lifestyle. She emphasizes the importance of self-care and balanced living, passionately advocating for an active and fulfilling life in retirement, ensuring the best years are ahead. Lara encourages readers to reclaim their vitality and joy at every stage of life.

Through her clear and structured writing style, infused with compassion and relatability, Lara makes complex health topics accessible and engaging, inspiring others to take charge of their health and well-being.

You can reach Lara via her website https://larawestbooks.com or Amazon Author Page https://www.amazon.com/stores/Lara-West/author/B0BV3F1YK7

LaraWestBooks.com

Amazon Author Page

Resources

Chapter 2.

Cost-Saving Tips for Retirees

These organizations provide resources, advocacy, and often discounts and services tailored to the needs of older adults.

1. **United States:** AARP (American Association of Retired Persons) (www.aarp.org) is the nation's largest nonprofit, nonpartisan organization dedicated to empowering Americans 50 and older to choose how they live as they age.

2. **United Kingdom: Age UK**(www.ageuk.org.uk). Age UK offers support, advice, and services to older people in the UK. They provide resources on health, financial advice, and offer discounts on products and services through partnerships.

3. **Canada: CARP (Canadian Association of Retired Persons**)(www.carp.ca). CARP is a national, non-profit organization that advocates for financial security, improved healthcare, and rights for older Canadians. They offer discounts on insurance, travel, and various services for members.

4. **Australia: National Seniors Australia**(www.nationalsenio

rs.com.au). National Seniors Australia is a leading advocacy group for older Australians, providing information on pensions, healthcare, and financial planning. They also offer discounts on travel, insurance, and other services.

5. **New Zealand: Grey Power** (www.greypower.co.nz). Grey Power is an advocacy organization representing senior citizens in New Zealand. It offers members discounts on a wide range of services and lobbies the government on issues like healthcare, pensions, and seniors' rights.

Medical Insurance:

1. **Medicare** (www.medicare.gov). For U.S. retirees, Medicare is an essential resource for medical coverage. Be sure to understand what is covered and consider supplemental plans like **Medigap** or **Medicare Advantage** to ensure you're fully protected, especially if you're traveling abroad where Medicare may not cover certain medical needs.

2. **Private Health Insurance Marketplaces** (www.healthcare.gov for U.S. residents). If Medicare doesn't fully meet your needs, private health insurance or supplemental plans might fill the gaps, especially for expats or retirees traveling internationally. Websites like **Healthcare.gov** help you compare private plans.

3. **Cigna Global Health Insurance** (www.cignaglobal.com). Ideal for retirees living abroad, Cigna offers international medical coverage, including access to global healthcare networks and coverage for both routine and emergency medical needs.

Insurance and Legal Considerations:

1. **International Driver's Permit (IDP)** (www.aaa.com or www.idpapp.com). If you plan on driving in a foreign country, an International Driver's Permit is often required. It's easy to obtain and valid in over 150 countries. Check the requirements for the countries you plan to visit to avoid legal complications while driving abroad.

2. **LegalZoom** (www.legalzoom.com). Offers online legal services for a variety of needs, including wills, estate planning, and legal advice related to international travel. It's a great resource for making sure your legal matters are in order before you head off on any adventures.

3. **U.S. Department of State – Travel Advisories** (www.travel.state.gov). Stay up-to-date with the latest travel advisories and legal considerations for U.S. travelers abroad, including information on international driving laws, visas, and health requirements in specific countries.

4. **Foreign Embassies and Consulates** (www.embassy.org or your country's government website). If you're traveling or living abroad, knowing how to contact your country's embassy or consulate is crucial. They can help with legal issues, lost passports, and emergency assistance.

Chapter 3.

Mindfulness and Meditation Retreats

1. **Spirit Rock Meditation Center (California, USA).** A renowned mindfulness retreat center nestled in the hills of Northern California. Spirit Rock offers a variety of retreats, from beginner mindfulness weekends to in-depth meditation

immersions. The center is known for its highly qualified instructors and peaceful, nature-filled environment.

2. **The Art of Living Retreat Center (North Carolina, USA).** Located in the scenic Blue Ridge Mountains, this retreat offers a blend of mindfulness, yoga, and Ayurveda. It focuses on stress reduction and self-care through guided meditation, breathing exercises, and holistic wellness practices. They offer programs ranging from weekends to week-long retreats.

3. **Shambhala Mountain Center (Colorado, USA).** Offering meditation and mindfulness retreats at an altitude of over 8,000 feet, this retreat provides deep spiritual teachings in a stunning, secluded mountain setting. Shambhala is known for its Buddhist-centered mindfulness practices and also offers yoga and tai chi.

4. **Plum Village (France).** Founded by Thich Nhat Hanh, Plum Village is one of the most respected mindfulness centers in the world. Retreats here focus on mindful living and peaceful, slow-paced meditation practices. Retreat participants experience silence, community life, and teachings that inspire mindfulness in everyday actions.

5. **Kamalaya Wellness Sanctuary (Thailand).** Set on the tropical island of Koh Samui, Kamalaya is a luxurious retreat offering a blend of mindfulness, yoga, and wellness treatments. It's perfect for those looking to combine meditation with relaxation and self-care in a stunning resort environment.

6. **Vipassana Meditation Centers (Worldwide).** Vipassana retreats are widely respected for their deep and immersive silent meditation programs. Typically lasting 10 days, these retreats are donation-based and focus on the traditional Buddhist

practice of Vipassana, or insight meditation. They are perfect for those seeking to dive deeply into meditation with no distractions.

7. **Esalen Institute (California, USA).** A unique retreat center on the California coast, Esalen offers mindfulness and meditation programs in combination with creative arts, personal growth, and bodywork. The stunning cliff side location and hot springs make it a perfect retreat for those looking to rejuvenate both body and mind.

8. **Gaia House (United Kingdom).** A silent meditation retreat center, Gaia House is set in the English countryside and offers mindfulness and insight meditation retreats. Their programs are led by experienced teachers and cater to both beginners and experienced meditators.

9. **Kadampa Meditation Centers (Various Locations).** Offering meditation and mindfulness retreats worldwide, Kadampa centers focus on Buddhist teachings and offer both silent and guided retreats. They're an excellent option if you're looking for a retreat closer to home with structured teachings and community involvement.

10. **Sivananda Ashram Yoga Retreat (Bahamas).** While primarily focused on yoga, Sivananda also offers mindfulness and meditation programs. This retreat allows you to combine your mindfulness practice with daily yoga, healthy meals, and time for beach relaxation.

Floating into Wellness: The Sensory Deprivation Experience

1. **Float On** – Portland, Oregon, USA https://floathq.com/

2. **London Float** Therapy – London, ON, Canada http://www.londonfloattherapy.com/

3. **Float House** – Vancouver, Canada https://floathouse.ca/

4. **Pause Float Studio** – Los Angeles, CA https://pausestudio.com

5. **Urban Float** – Multiple locations in the USA https://www.urbanfloat.com/

6. **Floatation Locations** – multiple locations in North America https://floatationlocations.com/where-to-float/

7. **Floatworks** – multiple locations in the **UK https://floatworks.com/**

Famous Hot Springs Spa Resorts

1. **Banff Upper Hot Springs (Canada).** Located in Banff National Park, this iconic hot springs resort offers stunning mountain views while you soak in mineral-rich waters. The temperature of the water remains around 98–104°F year-round, providing a perfect place to relax and relieve muscle tension.

2. **Blue Lagoon (Iceland).** One of the most famous hot spring spas in the world, the Blue Lagoon offers geothermal seawater rich in minerals like silica and sulfur, known for its skin-rejuvenating properties. The spa offers in-water massages and treatments in a serene, otherworldly setting surrounded by volcanic landscapes.

3. **Tabacón Thermal Resort & Spa (Costa Rica).** Nestled near

the base of the Arenal Volcano, this luxurious hot spring resort features natural thermal springs that flow through lush gardens. With multiple hot spring pools and waterfalls, it's a beautiful location to immerse yourself in mineral-rich waters, known to ease joint pain and muscle tension.

4. **Onsens in Hakone (Japan).** Japan is famous for its **onsens** (natural hot spring baths), and the Hakone region is one of the most popular spots. Surrounded by beautiful views of Mt. Fuji and natural landscapes, Hakone's onsens are known for their therapeutic properties, including reducing stress and improving skin conditions.

5. **Chena Hot Springs Resort (Alaska, USA).** For a unique hot spring experience, visit Chena Hot Springs Resort near Fairbanks, Alaska. The natural geothermal springs are famous for their healing properties, and on a clear night, you can even soak under the Northern Lights, making this a magical retreat.

Spa Retreats Worldwide

1. **Aman Spa at Amanpuri (Thailand).** Located in Phuket, this luxury spa retreat offers a wide range of treatments, including Thai massage, Ayurvedic therapies, and holistic wellness programs. It's an ideal destination for those looking to combine spa relaxation with cultural experiences.

2. **Rancho La Puerta (Mexico).** Situated just across the U.S. border in Baja California, Rancho La Puerta is a wellness-focused resort offering a mix of spa treatments, fitness classes, and mindfulness workshops. Their spa offers a range of treatments tailored to seniors, including massages and hydrotherapy designed to reduce arthritis pain and increase mobility.

3. **Ananda in the Himalayas (India).** Nestled in the Himalayan foothills, Ananda offers luxurious spa treatments based on Ayurveda, yoga, and meditation practices. The spa focuses on restoring balance to both mind and body with therapies aimed at rejuvenation and anti-aging.

4. **Canyon Ranch (Arizona, USA).** One of the most well-known wellness retreats in the U.S., Canyon Ranch offers a full range of spa treatments, wellness programs, and fitness activities. It's particularly renowned for its integrative approach, offering not just physical treatments but also health consultations, workshops, and classes to enhance well-being.

5. **Thermes Marins Monte-Carlo (Monaco).** Known for its cutting-edge anti-aging treatments, this luxurious spa is set on the French Riviera and offers a range of hydrotherapy treatments using seawater. Guests can enjoy thalassotherapy pools, steam baths, and saunas, all designed to detoxify and rejuvenate the body.

6. **Calistoga Ranch (California, USA).** Located in the heart of Napa Valley, Calistoga Ranch offers natural geothermal mineral pools combined with luxurious spa treatments, including mud baths and vinotherapy, which uses grape seeds and extracts to rejuvenate the skin.

7. **The Greenbrier (West Virginia, USA).** This historic spa offers a wide variety of treatments, including hydrotherapy, hot stone massages, and detox programs. The Greenbrier also features mineral baths sourced from local springs, known for their healing properties.

8. **Ojo Caliente Mineral Springs Resort & Spa (New Mexico, USA).** Ojo Caliente is one of the oldest natural health resorts

in the U.S., offering sulfur-free, geothermal mineral waters in a peaceful desert setting. The spa includes yoga classes, hot stone massages, and private outdoor soaking tubs.

9. **Terme di Saturnia (Tuscany, Italy).** This luxurious spa and thermal resort is known for its healing thermal springs, rich in sulfur and other minerals that are great for the skin and joints. The resort offers a wide range of wellness treatments, including thermal mud wraps and hydrotherapy sessions.

10. **Grand Resort Bad Ragaz (Switzerland).** Set in the Swiss Alps, this world-class resort offers thermal spa treatments using mineral-rich water from the Tamina Gorge. The spa specializes in health and wellness, offering personalized programs for rejuvenation and anti-aging.

11. **Thermae Bath Spa (Bath, England).** Located in the historic city of Bath, this spa uses natural hot spring water that has been used for healing since Roman times. The spa offers a combination of traditional treatments and contemporary spa therapies, all within a stunning rooftop pool setting.

12. **Lanserhof Tegernsee (Germany).** Nestled in the Bavarian Alps, Lanserhof is renowned for its cutting-edge medical spa treatments and detox programs. The spa offers everything from personalized wellness programs to relaxing massages, all within a scenic alpine environment.

13. **Brenners Park-Hotel & Spa (Baden-Baden, Germany).** Baden-Baden is famous for its therapeutic waters, and Brenners Park-Hotel & Spa makes the most of this natural resource. With its luxurious setting, this spa focuses on well-being, offering a range of hydrotherapy treatments, medical wellness programs, and relaxing massages.

Chapter 4.

Group Travel: Finding Retirement Travel Clubs

1. **ElderTreks (https://www.eldertreks.com/).** This company provides adventure travel specifically for people over 50. They offer small-group trips to off-the-beaten-path destinations for those seeking a more adventurous experience.

2. **Traveling Professor (https://travelingprofessor.com/).** A travel company that offers small group tours with a focus on cultural immersion, often including history, art, and culinary experiences.

3. **Overseas Adventure Travel (O.A.T.) (https://www.oattravel.com/).** Known for small group tours, O.A.T. offers immersive experiences in less-traveled destinations with a focus on cultural engagement.

4. **Grand Circle Travel (https://www.gct.com/).** Specializes in small group trips, cruises, and river cruises designed for seniors. They offer a range of itineraries across the world, including in-depth tours of Europe, Asia, and South America.

Solo Travel: Exploring the World on Your Own Terms

1. Road Scholar (www.roadscholar.org). Specializes in educational travel, offering a wide range of solo-friendly tours around the world, including immersive experiences in art, history, and culture. Road Scholar also offers solo travel resources, scholarships, and assistance in finding travel companions if desired.

2. ElderTreks (www.eldertreks.com). An adventure travel company exclusively for people aged 50 and older, offering small-group adventures and destinations worldwide. Solo travelers can easily join these groups, and ElderTreks offers options with no single supplements, making it budget-friendly for solo explorers.

3. Overseas Adventure Travel (O.A.T.) (www.oattravel.com). Specializes in small-group adventures and welcomes solo travelers, offering many trips with free or low-cost single supplements. The company focuses on immersive cultural experiences and includes both off-the-beaten-path and classic destinations.

4. Intrepid Travel (www.intrepidtravel.com). Offers small-group, adventure-focused tours worldwide. They welcome solo travelers on all trips, with many designed to encourage solo adventurers to connect with like-minded travelers. Intrepid also provides various itineraries suited for different physical abilities.

5. Solo Traveler Blog (www.solotravelerworld.com). A comprehensive online resource for solo travelers of all ages, featuring destination guides, safety tips, budget advice, and inspiring stories from other solo adventurers. It's especially useful for seniors seeking solo travel advice and inspiration.

6. Women Traveling Together (WTT) (www.women-traveling.com). WTT is a travel company specializing in small-group travel for solo women, particularly older women. It's perfect for female solo travelers looking for safety and companionship while still maintaining independence. They offer a variety of destinations worldwide.

7. Solo Traveler (National Geographic) (www.nationalgeographic.com/travel/solo-travel). National Geographic's travel site offers useful tips and inspiration for solo travelers, featuring everything from expert safety advice to recommendations on the best destinations for independent exploration.

8. Flash Pack (www.flashpack.com). Specializes in small-group adventures designed specifically for solo travelers in their 30s and beyond, with an emphasis on unique, off-the-beaten-path experiences. Ideal for seniors looking for adventure with a social element but also the independence of solo travel.

9. Traveling Alone Together (www.travelingalonetogether.com). A travel service that specializes in creating unique travel experiences for solo travelers, particularly women, with an emphasis on safety and community. Their trips foster a supportive and friendly environment, making it ideal for older solo travelers.

10. TripAdvisor Solo Travel Forum (www.tripadvisor.com/ShowForum-g1-i12357-Solo_Travel.html). An active online forum where solo travelers from all over the world share advice, ask questions, and offer tips. It's a valuable resource for gaining firsthand insight into solo travel destinations, safety concerns, and practical tips from fellow solo explorers.

Chapter 5.

Voluntourism

1. **Projects Abroad**: Offers a wide range of volunteer programs, including education, conservation, healthcare, and community development across various countries. (www.projects-abroad.org)

2. **GoEco**: Specializes in ecological and wildlife conservation projects, as well as community development and teaching.(www.goeco.org)

3. **Global Vision International (GVI)**: Provides ethical and sus-

tainable volunteer programs focused on conservation, education, and community development. (www.gvi.co.uk)

4. **WWOOF (World Wide Opportunities on Organic Farms):** Connects volunteers with organic farms worldwide, focusing on sustainable living and farming. (www.wwoof.net)

5. **Volunteer World:** A comprehensive platform offering volunteer projects in conservation, education, and social work, with reviews and detailed program information. (www.volunteerworld.com)

6. **Idealist:** Lists volunteer opportunities globally, including community development, healthcare, education, and more. (www.idealist.org)

7. **International Volunteer HQ (IVHQ):** Offers affordable and responsible volunteer programs in over 50 countries, from teaching to wildlife conservation. (www.volunteerhq.org)

8. **Earthwatch:** Focuses on scientific research and conservation projects worldwide, allowing volunteers to contribute to meaningful environmental work. (www.earthwatch.org)

9. **Habitat for Humanity:** Provides opportunities to help build homes for families in need in communities across the globe.(www.habitat.org)

10. **Global Volunteers:** Focuses on long-term sustainable development through education, health, and community-based programs. (www.globalvolunteers.org)

Cultural Exchange Tourism

1. **Cultural Homestay International (CHI):** Offers cultural ex-

change programs that include homestays, work and travel, and au pair experiences, providing immersive cultural engagement worldwide.(www.chinet.org)

2. **Global Citizen Year:** Focuses on cultural exchange through immersion in different countries, offering opportunities to engage in local communities through volunteer work and homestays.(www.globalcitizenyear.org)

3. **Friendship Force International:** Specializes in cultural exchange homestay experiences, allowing participants to live with host families and engage in meaningful cultural activities. (www.friendshipforce.org)

4. **Workaway:** Offers opportunities for cultural exchange by connecting travelers with hosts who need help in exchange for accommodation, with options ranging from farm work to language exchange and artistic projects. (www.workaway.info)

5. **WWOOF (World Wide Opportunities on Organic Farms):** Not only a great way to learn about sustainable farming but also an excellent cultural exchange experience where you live and work with local families. (www.wwoof.net)

6. **GoAbroad:** Provides a wide range of cultural exchange opportunities, including internships, volunteer programs, and language immersion, in destinations around the world. (www.goabroad.com)

7. **InterNations:** A global community that offers cultural exchange meetups, networking events, and opportunities to connect with locals and expatriates in cities around the world. (www.internations.org)

8. **Road Scholar:** Known for its educational travel, Road Scholar

offers cultural immersion programs specifically designed for older adults, allowing travelers to engage deeply with local customs and traditions. (www.roadscholar.org)

9. **The Experiment in International Living:** Offers immersive homestay and cultural exchange programs, including hands-on workshops in art, language, and local traditions. (www.experiment.org)

10. **Servas International:** A global peace and hospitality network that connects travelers with hosts around the world, fostering cultural understanding and meaningful connections through homestays. (www.servas.org)

Chapter 6.

Skydiving and Paragliding: Thrills in the Sky

Skydiving Organizations:

1. **United States Parachute Association (USPA)** www.uspa.org

2. **British Parachute Association (BPA)** www.bpa.org.uk

3. **Australian Parachute Federation (APF)** www.apf.com.au

4. **European Parachuting Union (EPU)** www.epc.pt

5. **Fédération Française de Parachutisme (FFP)** www.ffp.asso.fr

Paragliding and Hang Gliding Organizations:

1. **United States Hang Gliding and Paragliding Association (USHPA)** www.ushpa.org

2. **Paragliding and Hang Gliding Federation of Australia (SAFA)** www.safa.asn.au

3. **British Hang Gliding and Paragliding Association (BHPA)** www.bhpa.co.uk

4. **Fédération Aéronautique Internationale (FAI)** www.fai.org

5. **Swiss Hang Gliding and Paragliding Association (SHPA)** www.shv-fsvl.ch

Chapter 7.

Stargazing and Astronomy Clubs

1. **Dark Sky Festival (Utah, USA)**: Held in Bryce Canyon National Park, this festival offers some of the best night sky views in the U.S. Attendees enjoy ranger-led stargazing sessions, telescope viewing, and presentations from astronomers. The park's natural dark skies make it an ideal location for spotting planets, distant galaxies, and meteor showers.

2. **Texas Star Party (Texas, USA)**: One of the largest stargazing events in the U.S., the Texas Star Party takes place in the remote Davis Mountains. This week-long festival attracts amateur and professional astronomers alike and offers nightly star parties, workshops, and telescope viewings.

3. **Jasper Dark Sky Festival (Alberta, Canada)**: Held in Jasper National Park, a designated Dark Sky Preserve, this festival offers stunning views of the night sky paired with expert-led

stargazing tours, workshops, and even photography lessons. It's a fantastic way to combine outdoor adventure with celestial exploration.

4. **South Downs Dark Skies Festival (England, UK)**: Located in South Downs National Park, this festival celebrates the beauty of the dark night sky. The event includes stargazing sessions, astronomy talks, and opportunities to observe celestial events like meteor showers, all while enjoying the peaceful British countryside.

5. **Starmus Festival (Worldwide)**: Though not exclusively about stargazing, Starmus is an international festival that combines science, art, and music. With talks from leading astronomers and astronauts, stargazing sessions, and cultural events, it offers a broad exploration of the cosmos in various scenic locations around the world.

References

1. 200+ Bucket List Ideas for Retirement https://www.annuity.org/retirement/lifestyle/retirement-bucket-list/

2. How to Create a Retirement Budget https://www.ramseysolutions.com/retirement/how-much-money-will-you-need-in-retirement

3. Essential Digital Skills Evaluation Framework for Seniors https://officeforseniors.govt.nz/assets/documents/our-work/digital-inclusion/Essential-Digital-Skills-Evaluation-Framework-for-Seniors.pdf

4. Top 14 Travel Tips for Seniors [The Complete Travel Guide] https://blakeford.com/top-14-travel-tips-for-seniors-complete-travel-guide/

5. Outdoor Activities for Seniors with Limited Mobility https://www.seniorhelpers.com/mo/kansas-city-south/resources/blogs/best-springtime-outdoor-activities-for-seniors-with-limited-mobility/

6. The Health Benefits of Tai Chi for Seniors Aegis Living https://www.aegisliving.com/resource-center/the-health-benefits-of-tai-chi-for-seniors/

7. Mindfulness for Your Health: The Benefits of Living Moment by Moment https://newsinhealth.nih.gov/2021/06/mindfulness-your-health

8. Effects of Aqua Aerobic Therapy Exercise for Older Adults https://www.ncbi.nlm.nih.gov/pmc/articles/PMC3820233/

9. Senior Exercise Programs & Classes https://tools.silversneakers.com/Classes

10. Try Float Therapy at These Hotels and Spas Around the World https://businesstravelerusa.com/wellness/try-float-therapy-at-these-hotels-and-spas-around-the-world/

11. Learning To Play Golf At 60 https://www.golf-madness.com/blog/learning-to-play-golf-at-60

12. Reasons Why Skiing is Vital for Seniors https://snowvision.net/blogs/winter-sports-guide/reasons-why-skiing-is-vital-for-seniors

13. Positive aging benefits of home and community gardening https://www.ncbi.nlm.nih.gov/pmc/articles/PMC6977207/

14. 8 Best American Road Trips For Seniors https://www.roadscholar.org/blog/8-best-american-road-trips-for-seniors/

15. 2024 Best Travel Discounts For Seniors https://www.theseniorlist.com/senior-discounts/travel/

16. 9 Bucket List Cruises for Seniors and Retirees https://travel.usnews.com/features/bucket-list-cruises-for-seniors-and-retirees

17. Savvy Senior Travelers https://www.ricksteves.com/travel-tips/trip-planning/savvy-senior-travelers

18. Travel Insurance for Pre-Existing Conditions https://www.nerdwallet.com/article/travel/travel-insurance-pre-existing-medical-conditions

19. Binoculars and Beyond: Nine Tips for Beginning Bird Watchers https://www.allaboutbirds.org/news/binoculars-and-beyond-nine-tips-for-beginning-bird-watchers/

20. The Benefits of Hiking For Seniors https://www.hearthstoneseniorliving.com/blog/benefits-hiking-seniors/

21. Benefits of Nordic Pole Walking for Seniors https://seasonsretirement.com/nordic-walking-for-seniors/

22. The Blissful Benefits of Hot Springs https://www.theearthandi.org/post/the-benefits-of-hot-springs

23. A Senior's Guide to Geocaching: What Is It, Why Do It and Tips for Getting Started https://www.thegardensmo.com/blog/a-seniors-to-geocaching-what-is-it-why-do-it-and-tips-for-getting-started

24. The Ultimate Guide to Planning Your First RV Trip https://explore.bookoutdoors.com/guides/the-ultimate-guide-to-planning-your-first-rv-trip/

25. 9 Glamping Destinations Throughout the U.S.* https://www.aarp.org/travel/vacation-ideas/outdoors/info-2021/glamping-destinations.html

26. Participating in Activities You Enjoy As You Age https://www.nia.nih.gov/health/healthy-aging/participating-activities-you-enjoy-you-age

27. Online cooking classes with international chefs https://www

.thetablelesstraveled.com/cooking-classes

28. How to Build a Home Gym on the Cheap https://www.artofmanliness.com/health-fitness/fitness/how-to-build-a-home-gym-on-the-cheap/

29. World's 9 Best Places to Go Skydiving https://www.travelchannel.com/interests/outdoors-and-adventure/photos/best-places-to-go-skydiving-in-the-world

30. Age is just a number: Becoming a Scuba Diver after 60 https://www.richcoastdiving.com/post/scuba-certification-for-seniors

31. Motorcycle Touring for Beginners https://www.madornomad.com/motorcycle-touring-for-beginners/

32. Mountain Biking for Seniors: 5 Questions to Ask Before You Begin https://metalbladecycles.com/mountain-biking-for-seniors-5-questions-to-ask-before-you-begin/

33. How Safe Are Hot Air Balloons? (Solved) - Napa Valley Aloft https://nvaloft.com/2023/05/03/heres-what-you-need-to-know-about-hot-air-balloon-safety/

34. 13 White Water Rafting Tips for Beginners https://southeasternexpeditions.com/13-white-water-rafting-tips-beginners/

35. Your Best Ride is Ahead: Horseback Riding for Senior Citizens https://horserookie.com/horseback-riding-senior-citizens/

36. The 29 Best Glamping Resorts in the U.S. https://travel.usnews.com/features/top-glamping-resorts-in-the-us

37. The Top 16 Historical Sites in the World https://www.nomadicmatt.com/travel-blogs/ten-historical-sites/

38. 16 of the Best Ziplines Around the World https://backpackertravel.org/wanderlist/best-ziplines-around-the-world/

39. 20 Best Places for Wine Tasting Trips & Cruises for 2024-2025 https://www.adventure-life.com/activity/wine-tasting

40. Europe Themed or Special Events Tours 2024/2025 https://www.affordabletours.com/r/europe/spec/theme

41. 10 Best U.S. National Parks for Seniors to Visit https://travelingtulls.com/best-national-parks-senior-pass/

Also by Lara West

1. "Retirement Reinvented: Your Inspiring Guide to Creative Expression, Intellectual Growth, Entrepreneurial Ventures, and Leaving a Legacy for a Fulfilling and Meaningful Life After Work"

2. "The Ultimate Collection of Fun Things to Do in Retirement: Your Roadmap to Explore the World, Spark Creativity, Expand Your Mind, Uncover Hidden Talents, Make New Friends, and Savor Your Golden Years"

3. "7 Healthy Gut Habits For Women Over 40: Get Your Life Back Using Intermittent Fasting, Nutrition, and Self-Care to Restore Gut Microbiome for Weight Loss and Increased Energy"

4. "5 Pathways to Vagus Nerve Mastery for Women Over 40: Holistic Methods to Reduce Anxiety, Clear Brain Fog, Improve Gut Health, and Balance Weight During Perimenopause and" Menopause

5. "Gut Health Made Easy for Women over 40: Recipes to Revitalize Your Body and Mind, Manage Menopause Symptoms, Balance Hormones, and Lose Weight with Delicious Smoothies, Salads, and Soups"

6. "Joyful Transition For Women Over 40: Finding Gratitude and Thriving in Menopause with Empowering Affirmations, Journaling, and Positive Mindset Practices"

7. "The Ultimate Gut Health Collection for Women Over 40: Reclaim Your Vitality, Lose Weight, and Manage Menopause Symptoms with Intermittent Fasting, Self-Care, Balanced Nutrition, and Delicious Recipes"

8. "The Ultimate Mind-Body Harmony Collection for Women over 40: Reduce Anxiety, Clear Brain Fog, Improve Gut Health, and Thrive in Menopause with Vagus Nerve Mastery and Positive Mindset Practices"

9. "The Self-Care Guide for Dementia Caregivers: Proven Practices to Reduce Stress, Overcome Burnout, and Find Balance and Joy in the Caregiving Journey"

10. The Joyful Art of Swedish Death Cleaning: Declutter Your Home with Intention, Live Your Life with Simplicity, and Leave a Legacy Your Children Will Cherish

www.ingramcontent.com/pod-product-compliance
Lightning Source LLC
Chambersburg PA
CBHW071244070526
44583CB00017B/2314